THE
FISHERMAN'S
FRIEND

Ĺ

THE
FISHERMAN'S
FRIEND
A Bedside Companion

Bill Tidy and Derrick Geer

Lennard Publishing
1989

Lennard Publishing
a division of Lennard Books Ltd
Musterlin House, Jordan Hill Road, Oxford OX2 8DP

British Library Cataloguing in Publication Data
Tidy, Bill
The fisherman's friend.
1. Humour in English, 1945- Special subjects:
Angling - Anthologies
I.   Title   II.   Geer, Derrick
827'.914'080355

ISBN 1 85291 058 5

First published in 1989
© Bill Tidy and Derrick Geer

Editor Michael Leitch
Designed by Cooper-Wilson
Jacket design by Pocknell & Co
Typesetting by Wyvern Typesetting, Bristol
Printed and bound by The Bath Press

CONTENTS

VERY HONEST MEN

'This dish of meat is too good
For any but anglers,
Or very honest men!'

(Izaak Walton)

There are four million anglers in Britain. A handful of these know exactly what they're doing; a few more know what they're supposed to be doing and have almost got it right. The rest of us muddle by somehow.

An angler is a person whose perception of reality is at odds with the rest of the world. After all, the fish doesn't feel a thing. An angler is someone whose grasp of mathematics, particularly weights and measures, is erratic, his rule of thumb being 'double it and add a bit'. His concept of time is unreliable: 'Your dinner's ruined!' He can't count: 'We only stopped off for the one, dear.' And he is an optimist: 'Give it another couple of hours, and if there's still nothing doing we'll try over there. Bound to be better over there.'

The angler needs a sense of humour. 'Orf to drown a few worms this weekend then, Harry? Har, har, har!' But Harry doesn't mind. Your average angler is a tolerant sort. He wouldn't dream of pointing out to the scoffers the absurdity of grown men and women walking round a field trying to knock a little white ball down a rabbit hole with a stick.

The angler is almost unique in that he will spend more time discussing failure than he does success. The only other people known to do this in equal measure are the England cricket selectors. Your angler talks about the bad days to put the few good ones into perspective. It's not that he's complacent (unlike the England cricket selectors), it's simply that by the law of averages your angler spends a great deal more time actually not catching fish than he does catching them.

While pursuing his chosen hobby the angler is often wet, frequently cold, usually uncomfortable, occasionally miserable, sometimes sick. But he is never bored, and he will always come home, eventually, and say what a great time he's had. And he's only ever boring to those who fail to understand the immense pleasure to be derived from, for example, standing up to the armpits in a raging torrent which the local ducks have temporarily abandoned as being too dangerous.

Even without his rod and reel you can spot an angler from a mile away. If you tell him his flies are undone he automatically reaches up to his hat. Outside the fish shop he's the one, a faraway look on his face, stroking the scales of the big salmon laid out on the slab. In the crowded station bookshop at the height of the rush-hour he's the bloke scrabbling about on all-fours running his eyes over the fishing magazines on the bottom row, while all around him other blokes stand jostling each other and eyeing the contents of the top shelf.

In the Natural History Museum he's the Dad who drags his children off to the fish room when they want to see the dinosaurs first. Even in the pub he thinks a pint of the usual is a supply of maggots.

Four million is a fair-sized lobby. If we ever got organised we could change the world. But the truth is that anglers come from all walks of life, and apart from having a different set of priorities to normal people and a desire to catch fish the only thing they have in common is that they have very little in common. Put any two together and they have enough difficulty agreeing on the best bait for a particular day. If the need ever arose for a unified stand on really vital issues such as the place of Latin in the school curriculum, or the European Cocoa Quota, no chance!

However, all anglers might just about agree that although fishing, like money, isn't the reason for living, life would be a bit of a swine without it. Four million can't be wrong. Or can they?

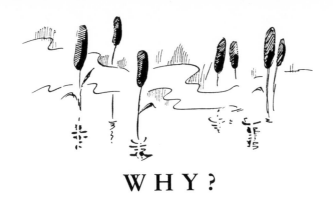

WHY?

'For every why he had a wherefore.'

(Samuel Butler)

Let's begin by examining a few motives and exploding several myths. ***Anglers like to catch fish.*** This is not a myth, and we can forget all that nonsense about being 'perfectly happy standing here all day long catching nothing'.

We've all heard it, some of us may even have said it, but nobody actually believes it. The next time you are having a lean session on the pier, or the canal, on a Sunday morning in midwinter with the cold rain trickling down your neck, and someone sidles up to you smiling sweetly and says, 'Do you know, I'm perfectly happy standing here all day long catching nothing,' tell him what you really think. And what he can do with his fishing rod. If you need convincing, just watch the expression on his face should you happen to catch something. A dinky dab or dace will change that sweet smile to paranoia in seconds.

Anglers catch fish to eat. This is largely a myth. There might be something in it, except that a coarse angler invariably puts all his fish back into the water before he packs up and pushes off home. And even though you may think that a successful fishing session for game or sea species does have an immediate end-product, most game and sea anglers of my acquaintance don't like eating fish and give away everything they catch. This strange behaviour doesn't seem to dampen their enthusiasm for the sport. On the contrary, these anglers are often among the most fanatical of fishermen.

Is the angler living out a role as ***Man the Hunter***? Is he answering some primaeval challenge? The call of Nature? The concept conjures up a noble picture. The reality is somewhat

different. My friend Jim is a nice bloke, salt of the earth, do anything for you. But hunched over his rods on the harbour wall of a Saturday in his greasy oilskins and flat cap, coughing his way through twenty 'full-strength', hands reeking of stale squid, you would hardly call him noble. A few adjectives might leap immediately to mind, but 'noble' is definitely not among them!

Escape is often mentioned as a motive. Getting away from the family for a few hours, particularly if the in-laws are coming for the day. On the other hand, escape can just as easily be achieved in other ways, such as going to the pictures or taking the cat to the vet, and it has to be said in their favour that these activities can be undertaken without risk of extreme discomfort and possible nausea. (Except in the case of the cat, of course.)

One flaw in the escape theory. Eventually your young son is going to want to come with you. Your wife's idea of when he is ready for this will differ from your own.

Wife: But you promised him!
You: He's only five, for God's sake!
Wife: He wants to go.
You: He's too young.
Wife: When then?
You: (Lamely) Soon. Eh?

Eventually, after weeks of this you take him with you. You might be going through a pier period, so it's lump-in-throat time as you proudly thread a worm for him.

'Ugh!' he shrieks. 'Tha's horrible. Don' like that. Poor worm!' While you try and fish with your rod, and his, he is busy stuffing your neighbour's ragworms through the pier planking.

'Don't do that, there's a good boy.'

He plays under the bench and gets a massive splinter in his hand.

'There, there. Better now.'

He knocks over your neighbour's rods.

'Come away! There's a good lad.'

He runs, trips, and nearly disappears over the edge.

'Stay right there! Where I can see you!'

And wants to go to the toilet.

'What, again?'

You finally give up and return home to find your wife halfway through a bottle of sherry, feet up, and having the best Sunday she's had for years. The first of many to come. Escaping is a two-edged sword!

Angling gives the fisherman the opportunity to savour the twin delights of *The Great Outdoors.* Fresh air and mosquitoes! Fresh air? Ever been on a deep-sea charter boat? Diesel fumes! And no matter how clean the deck may look the smell of old fish hangs around. A heady mixture, diesel fumes and rotten fish, and it clings.

I can't honestly say my nasal passages are exactly enamoured of certain stretches of the canal system either, particularly in what might once have been described as industrial areas. Fall into some of that stuff and you'd never play the violin again.

Of course there are areas where the air is clean and fresh, but it can often prove too much for the city dweller. One deep gulp can be a shock to the system, and many of you will have experienced the dry, hacking cough and sore throat that lasts for days until acclimatisation sets in, by which time the holiday's over and you're in the car on the way home.

Peace and Quiet. It is sometimes possible for the angler to find the sort of mind-numbing tranquillity that enables him to relax, to forget his everyday troubles. It's usually just as this state of calm has taken over that things start to happen.

The fly fisherman will find he's got a good rhythm going and he's reached the hypnotic state when there's a sharp tug on the line and he finds he's hooked into the dress of the woman walking along the bank behind him. A cliché, perhaps, but it does happen. I know!

'Get your hands off me!'

'Sorry. But please, do stop moving about. You'll bend the hook!'

Your coarse angler has just settled back to enjoy a quiet nap when an armada of canoeists, paddling like the clappers, appear round the bend and splash past, taking line from his rods as they go. He jumps up, has to cut the line to save his tackle, shouts at their retreating backs and angrily shakes his fist after them. They think he's being friendly, so they all wave back, smile over their shoulders and nod encouragement as they disappear downstream. This reaction does little for the angler's blood pressure.

In the boat out at sea the swell suddenly increases in a freshening wind. The boat begins to roll alarmingly and the angler has to jam his feet apart in order to stay on board. The rain starts pelting down, he hasn't got his waterproofs on, and the Skipper chooses that particular moment to locate the largest shoal of mackerel in thirty years.

On the beach your angler is just dropping off when he realises his tackle is snagged on rocks. While he deals with this an incoming tide sneakily throws a larger wave high up on the beach to swamp his tackle box and tip over his bucket of live crabs.

Meanwhile on the pier the angler is tucked snugly in his shelter, contentedly sipping hot tea when the lady with the poodles comes along. She bangs against his rods and they clatter to the floor, one of the poodles lifts a leg and piddles in the tub of lugworm, and at the same time the guy fishing a short way away yells out, 'There's a shoal down there! I can see 'em!' And he pulls in a line containing two large cod.

Angling is a relatively inexpensive hobby. It is **not**. The reason for this has a bit to do with boat fees, pier dues, rod-licences, fishing rights and club subs. It has a lot to do with **tackle shops**! Tackle shops are a major pitfall and should carry a government health warning. I do not know anybody who has ever entered a tackle shop needing two swivels actually come out with only two swivels. Everyone enters tackle shops with the best of intentions, but once inside our hands take on a life of their own.

'But it was a bargain, love. I need another reel and this was only £79, reduced from £81.'

'You didn't need another reel! You *wanted* another reel!'

'Well, yes. But I couldn't miss an opportunity like that, could I?'

'I despair! The kids need new shoes, the electricity bill is due any day (red version!), the car's in for its M.O.T. and it's bound to need money spending on it to get through, we haven't paid the milkman for five weeks! You're a selfish, self-centred beggar!'

'Yes, love. I know. But just come and have a look at it. It's got this little lever that...'

If you need to travel a bit to get to your fishing **transport** is another item of expenditure you will have to consider. At the end of an 'awayday' there are more heated discussions round pub tables concerning the petrol 'divvy' than about almost any other subject, and that includes the humanitarian motives of the present Tory government, and sex as a way to the top in the film industry.

Very occasionally
a group of anglers
will contain that jewel in
the crown, the man who
is determined to pay for
everything. 'It's all right, I'll
get these.' Such people are worth
encouraging, though it is easy to take advantage. 'You paying
again, George? In that case I'll have a treble this time.' And
George can be an embarrassment, particularly when he invites
everyone in for a nightcap at the end of a day during which he
has insisted on buying all the drinks and paying for the petrol,

and you're met in the hallway by his wife, in dressing gown and slippers, demanding to know what he's done with the Family Allowance Book.

When it comes to an actual vehicle your angler has a choice to make. The large estate car looks very nice in the driveway and it will accommodate all your tackle with ease. It will also accommodate everyone else's! While nobody minds doing their bit on a rota basis, with a vehicle like this you're going to find your name cropping up quite frequently, along with the attendant drawbacks, i.e. the excessive wear and tear inflicted on your sparkling upholstery by a bunch of fellows who aren't particular where they scatter the ash or what they've been treading in on the river bank, and, worse, having to sit po-faced sober in the corner while everyone else is up at the bar enjoying themselves.

As an alternative you might opt for a Mini, or even a Fiat 127 in the mistaken belief that with a car that small your name will have to come off the rota. This is misplaced optimism. Your angler is an expert at adjusting a pint to accommodate a gallon; he's had a lot of practice with most of the stories he tells! A Mini holds no fears. If it's got four wheels and an engine, they'll get everything in. Overloading? That's something Italians do with spaghetti.

Any angler foolish enough to invest in a minibus, carawagon or similar, deserves everything he gets.

When it comes to *bait*, many anglers can breed, dig or catch and freeze their own, but sooner or later, due to circumstances everyone is forced to buy some bait.

Jim and I were on a fishing holiday once, down on the south coast, and found ourselves having to purchase a few lugworm. Jim was astounded!

'How much?' he gasped at the man in the shop.

'£1 for ten,' said the man in the shop. 'Ten pence each.'

'Christ!' said Jim. 'I wouldn't have the nerve to sell my willy for that much!'

You can dress it up any way you like, and make all the excuses you want, but in the end it all comes down to one thing. Anglers like to catch fish, and all the rest is thinly disguised bull.

WHICH IS IT TO BE?

*'I have called this principle, by which
each slight variation, if useful is preserved,
by the term of Natural Selection.'*

(Darwin)

Somewhere along the line all the very best angling books make the point that the sport can be divided into three categories: Game, Coarse, and Sea.

Game fish are salmon, trout and sea-trout. Catching them involves the use of the least complicated equipment in the most expensive places. *Coarse* fish are the other freshwater species. Coarse angling is the art of making the simple as complicated as possible. *Sea* angling involves catching fish using any method short of gunpowder, unless you're serving with HM Minesweepers in which case you have the perfect excuse.

As a beginner the first thing you have to decide is which stereotype you most closely resemble. For example it's a well known fact that the game angler is a natural Tory; everyone knows that all coarse anglers vote Labour; and the sea angler, if he bothers at all, will support any party which declares its opposition to the imposing of VAT on lugworm.

If you eat dinner in the evening, read *The Times* and prefer a good malt to Tesco's Blended, then you're probably a candidate for game fisherman. You believe in conscription and refuse to believe anyone would actually call their son Darren. If you don't own a good stretch of river, you went to school with someone who does.

On the other hand if your favourite colour is dark green, and you're fairly convinced there must be a better use for a chicken carcass than making soup, then coarse angling could be the one for you, especially if you like being covered in badges. A coarse angler doesn't seem to mind going about looking like a mobile display unit advertising everything from the *Angling Times* to Cape Cod Fishfingers. If you've still got your schoolboy stamp album at home somewhere, and a pile of old *Eagle* comics under the bed which you won't let your wife throw out, then be doubly assured: you've made the right choice.

To qualify as a sea angler you eat 'snap' at midday (or midnight, depending on your shift), tea when you come home from work, and you have dinner once a week on Sunday afternoon when you get home from the pub. You drink Magnets Strong in a straight class, borrow the wife's brother's Chevette every time the petrol tank falls off your Cortina, and own a dog of indeterminate breed which can't keep its nose out of any food left below head height.

It's easy to think in terms of stereotypes, which is why we do it. Assistants in fishing tackle shops do it all the time. It's in tackle shops that the embryo angler first becomes aware of the pecking order. If you wander round the Game department you get called 'Sir' by the assistant and are accompanied everywhere. If you're taking a gander round the Coarse department the assistants leave you alone because they think you might know more about it than they do. Stray into the Sea Angling department and the assistant may, after a long pause and a very deliberate sigh, deign to look up from his copy of *Hot Rod*.

'Just looking, boys?' he inquires, pretty sure he already knows the answer.

'That's right, pal,' you reply. You don't want to disappoint him. Another sigh and his head goes back into the magazine.

To those outside the sport it might seem only natural that inside every sea angler there is a coarse fisherman bursting to get out, and that every coarse angler must have game fishing pretensions. Not strictly true. On the other hand, many sea anglers wish they had the coarse fisherman's money, and all coarse fishermen wish they had the game angler's style, but that's about as far as it goes. Most anglers are perfectly happy with their chosen area, and while they might attempt brief forays into the unknown, often with great enjoyment, they generally return gratefully to their original preference, rather like coming home from a holiday in Majorca.

Before you finally decide which it is to be, there are other factors to consider, and it must be admitted, sadly, that some of these are *social*. How would you feel, for example, about parking the BMW outside your local, The Royal Arms in Henley-on-Thames, one Sunday evening and entering the lounge bar to announce to a group of your chums, 'Hermione and I have had an absolutely super weekend on Skeggy Pier catching dabs on frozen squid!'? A conversation-stopper anywhere in Henley-on-Thames, I should imagine. It doesn't have quite the same ring as 'I bagged a nice brice of trite on Freddy's stretch of the Avon.' Alternatively, try a 'nice brice of trite' in The Foundry Welfare, Swinton, and they'd wonder why you've started to learn Rumanian.

Seasons. Bear in mind that game and some coarse fishing have seasons. These vary according to venue and may not fit your particular needs, much like a British Rail timetable. Sea angling has two seasons, good days and bad days – again, a bit like a BR timetable!

Geography. If you want to fish regularly it may not be practical to be always zooming off to the prime game rivers in the romantic wilds of Wales and Scotland. It might have to be the Leeds-Liverpool Canal, or Shoreham Harbour, your ambition and imagination held in check by geographical circumstance. You don't get many trout off Ramsgate; but then your committed sea angler would counter this by pointing out that the upper reaches of the Wye aren't renowned for their thornback rays.

Cost is what it often boils down to, but then if you can afford the coarse equipment needed to fish the Leeds-Liverpool properly you might almost be able to afford a rod licence for the Wye as an alternative, and you could save on expenses by sleeping in the back of your mate's ex-British Telecom van.

Finally *temperament*, and how do you view what you do. Game fishing is, by its very nature, a solitary activity. Your very presence on the bank, or in the water, stakes out a claim, an invisible but powerful barrier inside which no one else may safely stray without incurring wrathful looks, dark mutterings, and calls of 'My water, my water!' The game angler regards his sport as man against fish, a battle of wills, an intellectual struggle between equals. Now frankly I've always been a bit worried by this view of the relationship between myself and a trout so I tend not to subscribe to it, but then it must be said that it's a description that flatters some anglers. Incidentally, if you decide to become a game angler you have to remember that any fish is a 'he', as in 'He gave me a good fight,' and most important of all you must give the fish a 'sporting chance', though what on earth this means totally eludes me. The 'sporting chance' concept obviously eluded Owen Thomas as well!

FISHING FEAT

A seventy year old angler from Llanrwst in North Wales hung on to his 22 lb salmon even though the river bank collapsed and he joined the fish in ten feet of water. Owen Thomas took more than half an hour to land the fish in the River Conwy.

Sunday Times. 12.6.1988.

KEEP AN EYE ON THAT. I THINK I'VE JUST SPOTTED A NICE CHUBB!

Coarse angling can also be a solitary pastime, but more by design than accident. Your coarse angler will stake out his claim to ten feet of canal or lakeside much like a family does on a crowded Bank Holiday beach, and woe betide anyone whose shuttlecock lands in the prohibited area. He wants to be left alone to work out the logistics of it all on his slide-rule. The coarse angler regards himself as the boffin of the fishing fraternity. If the game angler is the Managing Director returning to his office two hours late after a damned good lunch, then the coarse angler is the firm's Technical Director who keeps a camp bed in the corner of the lab for late nights. He is an equipment freak who has so many tackle boxes it takes him half an hour to load them into the car. He takes everything with him except the kitchen sink, and the only reason he hasn't got that is because his wife was using it when he left home. The coarse angler will hold up an object that looks like a small aluminium teapot with lumps on it and say, 'Don't know how we ever managed without one of these. We must have been fishing in the Dark Ages!'

Sea anglers are the most gregarious of the three types. They're not particularly territorial, but on the other hand they can sulk with the best of them if someone beats them to their regular place on the pier.

Sea anglers tend to fish in groups. This is because:

(a) They consider it more fun that way.

(b) They might be thrown together on a charter boat and it's difficult to be standoffish when there's twelve of you having to suffer the decky's sense of humour!

(c) They travel together to keep down the cost, and

(d) They might need back-up if someone has pinched their regular place on the pier.

Sea anglers all hope the fish will give them a sporting chance, and all fish are 'buggers' as in 'Come here, you little bugger!'

Without descending into cliché it's all a bit horses for courses. You pay your money and you take your choice, even if it's Hobson's. But then a bird in the hand is worth two in the whatsits and everything will be hunky dory when the boat comes in.

NO MAN IS BORN
AN ARTIST

*'As no man is born an artist,
so no man is born an angler.'*

(Izaak Walton)

Tackle. Remember, there are lots of flies tied to catch fishermen, not fish! This applies to a lot of flash tackle you will see in the shops. It is the job of the assistant to make you spend as much money as possible, and if you've invested an arm and a leg in the 'Supra-Swish' fourteen-foot carbon job, and a reel with more gadgets than the flight deck of Concorde, then you're not going to have much left for other essentials such as a range of good hooks/flies/floats, some decent line, and drinks. Equally important, the actual cost of the fish you're likely to catch in your first season will work out more expensive per ounce than the current market value of gold.

Waders. A cautionary word. Make absolutely sure you get waders that fit properly; snug, but not so snug they make your voice rise several octaves when worn. And *adjust the straps carefully!*

Imagine, if you will, the eager angler carrying his gear across wet boulders to the water's edge. He slips, and one foot becomes jammed under a rock while the other carries on at top speed. As he falls the imprudently adjusted straps of his waders stretch, then rebound, pulling the top of the waders sharply upwards. He not only bites through his tongue, which is painful enough, but he also ruins his prospects. One fine morning, six months later, his wife returns from her ethnic pottery class at the Conservative Institute next to the library and declares, 'I'm not having any more!' This being the basis of her complaint, she leaves him, taking nothing with her save a few clothes and the ormolu clock given to them years ago by her Aunty Sissie.

He is of course devastated. He takes to drink and loses his job. His grown-up children refuse him access to the young grandchildren (for which he is not entirely ungrateful!), and eventually the building society re-possesses the house.

Incidentally, please bear in mind that sea anglers *never* wear waders on a boat. It doesn't matter how proud you are of the shiny new pair your wife bought you for your birthday. If other anglers see you wearing waders as you climb on board they may think you know something about the boat that they don't, and they may panic!

Bait. If you're off to the beach make sure you've got your own bait. Don't rely on the guy who says, 'I'll see you tonight then. Oh, and don't worry about bait. I've got plenty.' When you arrive you will find he's said the same thing to a lot of other people, and there are nine of you having to share three dodgy-looking lugworms stuck to a week-old bloodstained sheet of *The News of the World,* an ice-cream tub half full of mackerel which have seen better days, the skeleton of what was once a crab, and a couple of squid which have been in and out of the freezer so often that his wife has threatened to issue them with a rent book.

If it's maggots or worms you're into, and you're travelling, take some with you. The shop which you were hoping to buy from at your destination will have just run out. Actually, if you're in North Wales the shop will be shut! North Wales is the only place I know where the cafés close for lunch. If you were counting on the shop for bait then you can be sure that others will have done the same, and surely there can be no sadder sight in angling than half a dozen blokes, all geared up, sitting in a circle by a lakeside trying to convince each other that a game of I-spy is a better alternative to driving home.

Local Advice. Always listen to the locals and make allowances for their gift of understatement.

'Yurr! There do be a gurt little 'ole roit in front of 'ee!' This means that if you take one more step you will sink like a stone through icy river water to the bottom of a thirty-foot crater, your waders will quickly fill up, and if you're lucky they may find the body sometime around Christmas.

There will be times when you would be very willing to follow advice, but being new to the game you don't understand it, and you don't ask for fear of being thought ignorant, which you are.

'I wouldn't go round the cliffs if I was you. It's "springs" this week.'

Now you know damn well it's October and therefore by process of elimination it must be autumn, so you go round the cliffs and eventually find yourself cut off by the tide. You then have to choose between abandoning your gear, climbing to the top of the cliffs and getting back to base before nightfall; or alternatively dragging yourself and the gear up high enough to be out of harm's way and sitting it out. If you opt for the latter you will return to your car next morning to find that the

emergency services have been out
all night looking for you, and
when they find you sipping hot tea
and tucking into bacon sandwiches
in the harbour café they will be
very cross and use a lot of naughty
words to your face.

When the old fellow fishing
from high up on the steep, muddy
river bank says, 'It's a bit sticky on
the corner,' what he's really telling
you is that if you go over there you
will be up to your knees in evil
smelling goo within seconds.
After twenty seconds you
will be up to your waist
and settling down quite
nicely. At this point
your former life flashes
before your eyes and
you begin to wish you
had been kinder to
dogs.

If you are a romantic you will entertain fleeting notions of being rescued by the beautiful girl galloping the chestnut gelding across the nearby field. She will stop, you tell yourself, and pull you gently to safety with the aid of a scented silk scarf, and the two of you will ride off into the sunset towards her boudoir and who knows what pleasures.

What actually happens is that she sits astride the horse looking down at you from a great height while you grin sheepishly back and engage her in witty conversation. 'I see the FT Index is down again.' Meanwhile the old fellow fishing from high up on the bank has gone off, but not too quickly, to dig the farmer out of the pub, and he arrives half an hour later cursing you for an idiot, or worse. He eventually hauls you out of the mire by means of an old Massey Ferguson tractor and a length of thick, frayed rope, which cuts into the skin under your armpits.

However, there is no denying that, all things being equal, there is definite mileage to be gained from a natter with locals over a pint. Trouble is, locals and visitors often talk a different language. In a pub in Somerset, a visiting angler was chatting to a group of locals. They all seemed to be getting on well; locals giving out advice for all they were worth, the visitor, a retired Group Captain of World War Two vintage buying all the drinks. Finally the old boy started tapping his pockets.

'Any of you chaps got a pin?' he inquired.

The locals began fingering their lapels.

'You got a pin, George?'

'Nope! P'raps Silas has got one behind the bar. I could ask him if you like. Silas, you got a pin for the Group Captain?'

'No!' growled the Group Captain. 'Not a pin. A pin! I want to jot down a few notes!'

HANDY HINTS

(a) For the game angler

Imitating Nature. For game anglers in particular imitating nature is the key to success. The more you can imitate nature the better the results. But let's not go overboard about this! Floating downstream flat on your back pretending to be a log might prove several things, but it's no guarantee that you will catch many fish, and you may end up having rocks thrown at you by Boy Scouts as you drift past their campsite.

Maps. Fishing for salmon, sea and brown trout in the very best waters is still for the relatively well off, but it is sometimes possible to buy day/week tickets. These will have a map on the reverse purporting to show you where you may fish. Unfortunately, unless it's a map of a very small lake or reservoir, this will bear no resemblance whatsoever to any stretch of countryside you're ever likely to encounter. They are usually printed in black and white. All well and good, except that railway lines look like roads, and rivers look like both. The 'key' of the map is handwritten in a tiny scrawl designed to be totally incomprehensible. They'll take your money but they don't want you to find their fish. Even if you've got the map the right way up this doesn't necessarily mean you're going to get where you want:

'Sorry, Sir, but you can't fish here!'

'But my map...!'

'Never mind your map, Sir! This is private water. Moreover it happens to be a fish farm.'

'Fish farm?'

'That's right, Sir.'

'Blimey! I thought I was doing rather well!'

A Good Summer. This is a relative term and means different things to different people. For example it is generally considered a waste of time and money to fish for salmon and sea trout in prolonged dry, rainless periods, and therefore you must not let the bucket-and-spade brigade among your fellow hotel guests hear you praying for rain. They will send you to Coventry. In the bar after dinner they will make a point of not coming up to you to tell you what a fascinating day they've had touring a local pottery, and what is worse they won't let their children show you the pictures they drew while stuck indoors all day because of the appalling weather, which appeared out of the blue at *your* instigation. And it's no good you trying to explain that you only wanted a little bit of rain, and that the floods which now cover seven counties have ruined your holiday as well.

Flash. Fly fishermen in particular have to be very careful not to give away their presence to the fish. On a sunny day, for example, it is not a good idea to use a highly polished rod since it is possible for the little blighters to see a flash before you can get near them. If you want to be serious about this, you will also have to consider the glint of sunlight on your specs, so get fitted with contact lenses. And the dull gleam of your dentures? Better to whip them out before you start. If your knees are prone to the odd click-click now that you're getting on a bit, bandage them heavily to cut down on noise. Try not to mutter to yourself, e.g. 'Let's see how you like this one, you little devil!' and the chunk-chunk emanating from the earphones of your Sony-Walkman is a dead giveaway.

Wet and Dry. Right at the start learn the difference between wet and dry lines/flies. A dry fly that ought to be merrily tap-dancing over the surface of the water is not going to attract many fish if it's being dragged, gasping for air, under the surface on the end of a sinking line. Alternatively your wet fly, deliberately designed by clever men who know exactly what they are doing, to imitate a drowning fly, looks a bit suspicious whizzing about enjoying life to the full up top.

Night Fishing. Sooner or later someone's going to flop down on the bar stool next to you, grab your arm in dramatic fashion, and whisper urgently, 'Remember! The darker the night, the darker the fly!' This may well be a sea-trout man talking, but the best course of action is to leave. After all, if it's going to be that dark, where's the fun in that? Life is complicated enough as it is.

Idle Talk. When fishing, it pays to check who you're chatting to. An unfortunate acquaintance settled himself onto the bank one day, began fishing, and in between engaged himself in idle conversation with the angler next door. For half an hour he regaled his neighbour with advice on the best way to get under-size and other illegal catches away from the river and safely home, even illustrating the technique at one stage with a small trout. It was at this point that the other man declared himself to be an Honorary Bailiff, produced his warrant, and asked for the offender's name and address. Idle talk can cost much more than lives. It may cost a hefty fine and a lost licence. Serves him right.

(b) For the coarse angler

Too Much! Believe it or not, even as a coarse angler you can overdo the equipment!

'Now, let's see. What have we got here? Pinkies, squats, maggots, frozen faggots. Live bait, dead bait, groundbait, masticated cheese. Bread paste, slug paste, paste sandwiches. Drop net, keep net, hair net, hooks. Floats, feathers, weights, reels and brolly, and my little plastic model of the Eiffel Tower. Quiver tips and chairs, tools and glue for running repairs. Wigglers, wogglers, wagglers, and a packet of things. Etc., etc., etc. Right! I think that's about it.'

'Shall I start running this lot down to the bank?'

'Good idea, Bob. I'll bring the rods.' Pause. 'Um...Bob?'

'Yes?'

'Where are the rods? What have you done with the rods?'

'I haven't done anything with them. You said you'd bring them.'

'That was just now.'

'I know.'

'I mean before.'

'Before what?'

'Before we left home! What did you do with them?'

'Nothing! You said check this lot and get it...'

'Sod it! Don't tell me you've actually managed to forget...!'

'Now hang on a minute! It was you who said...!'

This is an example of 'woods for the trees'. In the circumstances a posh mahogany box containing almost seven hundred floats is going to be no use whatsoever, unless you plan to spend the rest of the day playing Pooh-sticks!

As a novice coarse angler you will come under a lot of pressure to purchase bits that you really won't need until you become more expert at the basics.

'You mean you ain't got one of these?'

'No. What is it?'

'Haven't a clue. But the bloke in the shop says everyone's buying them so I wouldn't be seen dead without it now.'

The Audience. All anglers encounter The Audience sooner or later, and nobody likes it. As a coarse angler you're going to get a lot of it, particularly where a footpath runs along the river bank or the canal. The Audience takes many forms, but it's most often the old man with a small mongrel dog, and a little boy with a runny nose. Like spectres at the feast they appear suddenly from nowhere, and they wait, watching, silently demanding to be entertained. The old man may eventually growl, 'Any luck?' You shake your head. He then grunts knowingly. There is a long pause. It's now that you'll start to feel inadequate, as though you ought to be pulling one in at this very moment for their benefit, but of course nothing happens so you begin to feel guilty. Another awkward pause. This is when you should do the sensible thing by turning round to say, 'Look, why don't you bugger off and go and annoy someone else?' but instead you opt for the honourable way out by telling lies.

''Course it's usually pretty good on this stretch,' you venture.

'Oh aye!' He makes it sound like an accusation.

'Pulling them in by the ton yesterday.'

'Oh aye!'

'Masses of them.'

'Oh aye!'

There's nothing more to be said. You sit hunched miserably over your rods, feeling their eyes boring into the back of your head. You might begin to whistle nervously to yourself to keep your spirits up, but the worst thing you can do is to look round again because you will only receive a blank stare and an upward twitch of a shaggy eyebrow, and you may feel compelled to babble again. The best course of action is merely to sit it out. It will be hard, but having achieved their objective, i.e. making you feel like a fraud and an incompetent, they will eventually move on to play the game with another poor bloke.

Guilt. When, in your early matches, your line gets tangled up with those either side of you, and it will, *never admit that it's your fault!* They're going to blame you anyway, so you may as well learn to stick up for yourself right from the start.

The Catapult. This will be your second catapult. It will bear very little resemblance to your first, the weapon your Dad made for you out of a hazel branch when you were ten, but the end results will be similar – inaccuracy, torn fingernails, and sore ears. It always looked so easy in *The Beano*. You may not be convinced that you need a catapult, but try telling this to the man in the shop.

'Essential, Sir, your catapult!'

'Essential?'

'For ground-baiting, Sir.'

'Couldn't I do it myself, by hand?'

'Bring you out in spots, Sir!'

A Place for Everything. Always return all items of gear to their proper place. This applies particularly if you fish in a regular group or club and share a tackle box.

An angler took his friend along to one of his club sessions on a quarry reservoir in the North. He introduced him to the members in turn, and finally arrived at a pleasant-looking little man wearing a T-shirt bearing the legend 'Coarse Anglers Do It At Every Opportunity: Apply Within'.

'Dave Roberts,' said the angler. 'Only we call him Pickfords.'

'Pickfords?'

'Yes, he's always moving things!' came the reply through gritted teeth.

A Man's Gotta Do! One day, when you are young and at your most vulnerable, you'll come across him. He'll be looking over your shoulder as you push the maggots round the tub with your finger, trying to find the big ones at the bottom.

'Cold mornings,' he says, 'Cold mornings I generally pop a few in my mouth. Gets 'em warmed up and squiggling a bit.'

You look up incredulously, but he's already sauntering away.

Could this be it? you ask yourself. Could this be the ultimate test of manhood? Well, you've tried just about everything else; getting whizzed up on three halves of lager and locking yourself in the wardrobe as you tried to find the bathroom in the dark; being sick over your Dad's runner beans after smoking a whole packet of untipped cigarettes; nearly making it with Sally Brompton, and you would have too if her Mum hadn't come in and thrown a bowl of potato peelings over you! Child's play! Putting maggots in your mouth is obviously what it's all about.

So you pick up one of the little squirmers and lay it gingerly on your tongue. Not too bad. How about another? Pretty soon you've got half a dozen in there and you softly close your mouth so they can't escape. You're not exactly enjoying the sensation, but at least you're now a real man. So what comes next? What comes next is that the bloke who started all this arrives quietly, unexpectedly behind you, slaps you heartily on the back and says, 'How's it going then? Caught anything yet?'

Gulp!!

It's a funny thing, but ask yourself this. Have you ever seen anyone who says they put maggots in their mouth, actually doing it?

(c) **For the sea angler** (Beaches and piers)

Tide Tables. Read tide-tables very carefully! This applies particularly if you are travelling some distance.

After driving through the hours of early morning two fishermen, Jim and Bob, arrived at daybreak on a notorious beach in the south-west of England, all geared up and keen, to find the sea a mile out over thick grey mud, and still disappearing.

'Bloody hell!' said Jim, throwing everything he was carrying to the ground in disgust. 'I've seen more water in a pair of socks after they've been through the spin dryer!'

Another angler set out from Walsall with a group of friends to fish a bridge crossing one of the huge estuaries on the west coast of Wales. When they arrived they found the tide out, and the bridge spanning nothing but vast acres of dry, yellow sand. There was nothing else to do but repair to the pub on the wall of the nearby harbour. This was also dried up for the day (the harbour, that is, not the pub). The locals had a field day!

First Local: What d'you suppose it is they were hoping to catch, Gareth? Camels, is it?

Second Local: No, Bryn! Haven't been a camel caught round here for nearly six years.

First Local: Oh! Well, let me guess then, boys. No, no! Don't tell me! I bet you're the cast for the new production of 'The Desert Song' up the village hall, is it?

After an hour of this the group could take no more and they left for home.

Fishing at Night. If you're fishing from the beach at night, check the level of oil in the lamp before you set out. The foolish virgins didn't, and look what happened to them! The beach is no place to be in the pitch dark with a gang of 'gung-ho' anglers all intent on slinging baited hooks as far out to sea as they possibly can. There are more sharp hooks whizzing about than there are flies in a Scarborough carsey. In such conditions a hook is bound to get you eventually. If you do manage to pull your head back sharply to avoid the one that zips past your eyes, the next one will sink into the back of your knees.

It's also important to leave vital pieces of equipment near the lamp where they can be seen and found. There is nothing more terrifying than to have a large thornback ray lashing around your legs while you scrabble about on all fours in the near dark, twenty yards from the lamp, desperately trying to find the pliers.

Spinning. This is a very effective method of catching some game and coarse species given the correct conditions, but don't believe everything the experts say about this method of catching sea fish! You will read reports in books and magazines that run something like this:

After just a few minutes this shore mark began to prove really productive. We tried a variety of spinners, but once again the most deadly turned out to be the little 'Gold Top', always a favourite of mine. I never leave home without having one of these little devils tucked away somewhere in the old box. When all else fails they rarely let me down, and are used to best effect with line of no more than $\frac{1}{2}$ lb breaking strain. And so it was to prove on this particular day. Within half an hour we had beached seventy-two bass to 12 lb.

With his usual good fortune Arnold also hooked a huge tope, attracted to the shore by the feverish activity, but unfortunately he lost it! Dear old Arnold became so excited as the tope began to strip line from his reel that he had a heart attack and dropped down dead on the spot! As a mark of respect to our friend we sadly agreed to cut the line, and this magnificent creature sped away to fight another day. Meanwhile the fish were still biting, so we decided to carry on fishing and to deal with Arnold later. After all, it's what Arnold would have wanted. So we returned once again to our sport. The fish were literally kicking lumps off each other in their frantic attempts to get in close and grab our little 'Gold Tops'.

The truth is, you can try spinning from all kinds of shore marks, and the only thing it will produce is a mackerel which has lost its way, and a black plastic dustbin liner full of soggy garden rubbish. Mind you, the latter can be pretty exciting until you find out what it is!

(d) For the sea angler (Boats)
Keep the Skipper Happy! Forget everything you may have heard about how you are paying for a service and are entitled to *x*, *y* and *z*. Once you're on board the Skipper can do anything he likes with you. So keep him happy, even if you have to resort to sycophancy. Ingratiate yourself at every opportunity.

'Oh, what a lovely boat,' you should say. 'I'm in this little tight corner over here am I, Skip? Next to these old mackerel tubs. Super!'

Should you fail to keep the Skipper happy you could find yourself anchored four hundred yards off-shore over the same non-productive mark for a full ten hours while he catches up on some sleep in the cabin. Incidentally, beware of *levity*. As you come aboard do not greet your Skipper with 'Hello, sailor!' He didn't think it was funny when he first heard it, twenty-seven years ago.

Knife. Never get on board with a new filleting knife in a clean sheath. Everyone will immediately know you are a beginner. Dirty the sheath before you arrive at the quayside. I recommend rubbing down with equal parts old engine oil, soil from the garden, and grit from the bottom of the budgie's cage. This treatment will give your knife the lived-in look overnight. Further on the subject of knives: under no circumstances is it wise to borrow a fishing knife without asking the permission of the owner first. Borrowing a fishing knife without asking the permission of the owner first is regarded as a cardinal sin. It's regarded almost as shocking by boat anglers as you wanting to sleep with their wife. (Actually, a lot of boat anglers would rather you slept with their wife!)

Fishing Smock. A new smock can also be a dead giveaway. Before you wear it, a new smock should be put through the washing cycle at least ninety-four times, ninety-five if you want

HE WONT LIKE YOU BORROWING HIS FISHING KNIFE AS WELL!

to err on the side of safety. The desired effect can be further enhanced by tearing a seven-inch rip in one of the sleeves. This will show where the last porbeagle shark you caught nearly tore your arm off as you were returning it to the water. And never sew new badges onto a smock that is now rendered acceptably tatty. New badges should be left outside on a windowsill in a sunny position for at least three months before being transplanted onto your smock.

Know Your Place. For instance, should there be only one fresh mackerel on board for bait, precedence must be given to the more senior anglers. Generally it is The Skipper who decides the order of priority! Yes, it may mean that you end up fishing for tope with a bony piece of mackerel spine the size of a rock-goby's testicle, but it's better than nothing. At least, the rock-goby thinks so!

Seasick. Never loftily declare for the benefit of all on board, 'Oh, I'm never sea-sick, you know.' This only guarantees that you will be throwing up over the side within five minutes.

Handling Fish. If you're not sure how to handle a fish you've caught, don't be afraid to ask for help. The more experienced angler next to you will be only too pleased to receive an invitation enabling him to illustrate his expertise in dealing with the rasping skin of a dogfish, or the vicious spikes of a large bass. And anyway, you can live with being thought a wimp! Also, don't ask the decky to gaff your very first fish, that little 10 oz dab you have brought so proudly to the surface. It really isn't necessary. In fact never ask the decky to gaff anything under 50 lb. He will regard any such request as a slur upon his manhood, and a telling comment on your skills. On the other hand don't be silly and go to the other extreme. You don't prove much by refusing all help with an 80 lb conger eel; only that you are an ignorant plonker and a dangerous man with whom to fish!

Casting! Always remember a cramped charter boat is no place to show off your lengthy beach cast using the pendulum method. Someone tried early one morning when the fishing party were on the first mark of what promised to be an excellent day. Before anyone realised what he was doing, he was in full swing! Everyone dived to the floor for cover, but even so, as the hook whizzed across the deck it took a sizeable chunk out of somebody's ear. Ears being what they are, this one bled so profusely that the Skipper upped anchor immediately and headed for home in case the wound needed stitching. He could see the headlines: 'ANGLER BLEEDS TO DEATH WHILE SKIPPER FISHES ON.'

We all protested at having to finish our day prematurely. This protest included the injured party who appeared perfectly happy with the galley teatowels we'd wrapped round his head. All the way back the poor man who had caused the injury kept telling everbody how sorry he was, and how it was his first time on a boat and he hadn't realised, and how badly he felt about it all. Needless to say, being the type of people we were, we all rallied round to make him feel a lot worse!

TRUTH, SIR,
IS A COW!

'Truth, Sir, is a cow which will yield such people no more milk, and so they have gone to milk the bull!"

(Samuel Johnson)

*T*hings People Say. One of the first requirements of the complete angler is that he should be able to distinguish fact from fiction, if not in his own stories then at least in those of fellow anglers. Anglers never lie, but they are expert at disguising the truth. For example when the old boy in the pub says, 'You should have been here last week!', what he really means is, 'We didn't catch anything last week either!'

What they say	What it really means
Phew! I'm into something really big!	He's snagged on some rocks. (*You* know it, *he* knows it, but he's not going to admit it!)
I caught a lovely plaice last time I fished here.	He caught a small flounder last time he fished here.
Damn it! Missed him!	He was asleep.
I can definitely feel something nibbling away down there.	The lead is bouncing on the bottom.
I have a little man in Wales who ties all mine specially for me.	He gets them from his wife's Littlewoods catalogue.
It's a bit lumpy out there, but we should be all right. (The Skipper)	It's blowing a hurricane and you're all going to be sick as dogs!
It was a fantastic day, dear.	(*a*) It only rained in the morning. (*b*) The fags lasted out. (*c*) He didn't catch anything. (*d*) They stopped at the pub on the way home and he's whizzed up!
Of course, I've got a multiplier reel at home but I find a fixed-spool reel more effective on this stretch of beach.	He can't cast with a multiplier reel without getting a bird's nest the size of a football.

Now that's what I call a fish!	It's a fish. Much like any other.
A smashing day, Skipper. The lads have enjoyed it. I'll be in touch soon about another one.	You're a lousy skipper, your boat stinks, and we're going to try somewhere else next time.
I've won the club's Best Angler trophy three years on the trot.	The club secretary is his brother-in-law.
It was so big it broke the line.	He hadn't tied the knot properly
Well, it certainly gave a good account of itself.	It got away. (Probably because he hadn't tied the knot properly.)
The Skipper reckons it may have been near the record.	It was so small the Skipper threw it back without bothering to weigh it. This put the angler into a sulk so the Skipper had to say something nice to appease him. (The deck hand hadn't been round to collect the money yet.)
Yes, plenty of bait left. There's maggots in the tin there. Help yourself. No, of course I don't mind.	Parasite!
Feels a bit lively. Could be bream.	It's a dogfish!

The landowner's a bit of an eccentric, but I get on all right with him.	The farmer's a grumpy old sod who thinks you're a dummy.
We won't need the umbrella.	You're going to wish you'd taken the umbrella.
Right, lads. Reel in! There's not much doing here so we'll move on. (The Skipper)	Everybody's catching fish, but he's bored and wants something to do.
The water bailiff and I are old chums.	He's scared witless by the water bailiff, just like the rest of us.
NO FISHING FROM THIS SECTION OF THE HARBOUR WALL! (Council Notice)	The flash gits with the power boats, water skis and wetsuits can afford to pay us more than you plebs!

A MAN SO VARIOUS

*'A man so various that he seemed to be
Not one, but all mankind's epitome.'*

(John Dryden)

As with other forms of sporting activity the angler falls
conveniently into a category, an easily recognisable 'type'.
This should not be confused with stereotyping, being a much
more sophisticated exercise, involving total belief in yourself as
normal while everyone else is not.

GAME ANGLERS

The Colonel. Sometimes referred to as *moribundus*, The
Colonel is to be found on river banks taking a black labrador

for a walk, or in the
lounge bar, gin and
tonic in hand, elbow
placed carefully on
the mantelpiece for
best dramatic effect.

The Colonel is a local and lets everyone know it, not with any open show of ostentation, but subtly, by calling out to the landlord in a very loud voice, ''Nother one over here when you're ready, Bob!' Nobody has ever actually seen The Colonel fishing, but he wears a hat bristling with flies, and he drops hints in hushed tones about the 30 lb salmon in the case over the bar. 'What d'you reckon to that little beauty then, eh?' And he winks conspiratorially, but will say no more. 'Say no more! Own trumpet and all that sort of thing.' At the drop of a hat he will give you the benefit of his vast local knowledge whether you've asked for it or not. The sport's not been the same since they invented the Devon Minnow, and his favourite expression is, 'You should have been here last week, old boy!'

Eager Beaver. Eager Beaver is a bit of a one-man disaster area. He thrives on the theory that if you're keen enough everything else will follow naturally, and that includes any skills that might be required. Unfortunately 'keen' in his vocabulary is synonymous with 'frantic', and most of what he does is frantic.

193... 194... 195...

It's only by exercising extreme restraint that he doesn't actually scream 'Geronimo!' as he stumbles into the river, thrashing about to left and right with rod and line. Give him a sledgehammer and he'd be equally happy, and just about as effective as he crashes about among the boulders, a huge grin on his face, body and waders moving completely independently of each other. The Eager Beaver wouldn't know a contemplative moment if it came up and introduced itself, and if he doesn't retreat from the river in the evening feeling thoroughly shagged out, physically if not mentally, then it's all been a dreadful waste of time. His cavortings do not make him a popular figure among fellow anglers since his main claim to success lies in scaring away all living creatures, in or out of the water, over a ten-mile radius.

Why on earth he's taken up fishing you will never know. His personality would seem to be much better suited to an energetic game of squash, or membership of the SAS. Possibly both at the same time! He will phone you up in the middle of the night wanting to know if you've got anything on for the first Thursday in September in two years' time.

'I've booked a lake in Derbyshire for the day. Thought a few of us might club together. Can you let me know now?'

The Loner. The Loner considers himself to be the aesthete of the fishing fraternity, able to appreciate the finer things in life. For a start he's the only angler who doesn't get into a muck-sweat at the approach of the water bailiff. You know? That familiar feeling of panic that you might be doing something wrong, although you know perfectly well you're not! Like you get when you're being followed down the motorway by a

FOR GODS' SAKE, KEEP STILL!

police car. Such emotions don't bother The Loner; he's far too busy composing an ode to a Hairy Mary. To him fishing is a poem, to be enjoyed in splendid isolation, preferably at a time of day when sparrows are enjoying their first scratch. The Loner's already on his way home, two nice fish tails protruding from his bag, when the rest of us are arriving amid a morning chorus of banging car doors, muttered curses at last night's excesses, and fervent prayers that we won't have to deal with anything too lively till we've woken up properly.

'Couple of nice looking fish there, mate,' you remark.

He will smile modestly. 'Non multa, sed multum,' he breathes.

'A la carte!' you reply. 'Défense de fumer!'

Freddy Fly. If The Loner is an aesthete, Freddy Fly considers himself the aristocrat of angling. He's not a real aristocrat, of course, though he might be, but he's just as likely to be a plasterer from Peckham. Freddy's claim lies not in birthright, but in the fact that he refuses to believe that there's any other way to catch fish than by use of the fly, and any fish that can't be taken that way isn't worth catching anyway. Fly fishing is man's ultimate achievement; never mind the space shuttle, the Sistine Chapel, and free school dinners. Fly fishing is the reason we are all here. Spinners, spoons and Devons? He reserves the same kind of scorn for those who would resort to such barbarism as the rest of us might do for people who kick dogs or drink Australian lager. (Any lager come to think of it!)

Naturally Freddy ties his own. There isn't a parrot, peacock, cockatoo or domestic chicken living near Freddy which sleeps sound in its bed at night for fear of the hand through the bars.

Freddy writes a column about fly-tying in the Parish Magazine under the by-line 'Muddler' which he thinks is an in-joke which will be appreciated by the initiated, but this only serves to illustrate what a smart-arse he is, since nobody understands the rest of the column either. The only other keen angler in the parish is the Verger and he's a sea angler and quite beyond the pale. For every hour he spends fishing Freddy spends at least ten tying flies, and when he's not tying them he's thinking about them. The last time his wife got a sensible answer to the question, 'What would you like for breakfast, dear?' was thirty years ago just as Freddy was beginning an article entitled 'Fly Tying as a way of Life' in the *Daily Herald*. Nowadays his wife's favourite expressions are, 'Yes, dear. Very nice,' and 'Are you sure you should be doing that in this light? It can't be very good for your eyes.'

Great Aunt Maud. Great Aunt Maud is to be found exclusively in fast-flowing rivers in Scotland. She is one of the 'gels', or at least she was back in 1926 when she drove a London omnibus in the General Strike. Great Aunt Maud is a spinster, by choice, since she considers a 20 lb salmon on 6 lb line to be much more of a challenge than any man she's ever met and certainly loads more fun. She complains about the lift in the hotel not working between its two floors, but thinks nothing of trekking three miles every day to her favourite stretch of the river over the roughest terrain and through the foulest of weather. Rain or shine she wears her ankle-length Barbour, green wellies and deerstalker hat, her one concession to fashion being the brown silk scarf covered in pictures of leaping fish which she saves for special occasions, and a tiny enamel Cross of Lorraine, discreetly pinned under a lapel, a memento of her time behind enemy lines in the last war.

To her nephews and nieces, not one of whom is remotely interested in fishing, she sends an annual subscription to *Trout and Salmon* at Christmas, and *Game News* on their birthdays. (Although one year, due no doubt to some sort of computer error, Melissa started receiving copies of something entitled *Gay News*, and she's not been the same since!)

Great Aunt Maud treats ghillies as equals, waiters with disdain, and anyone who uses any line above a 10 lb breaking strain with contempt. Marie Stopes was a saint, Salome had the right idea but went a bit over the top, Lady Macbeth was a philistine for agreeing to marry the weed in the first place, and if God had intended women to have babies and stay at home she wouldn't have given them minds. Great Aunt Maud's favourite expressions are:

(*a*) Magnificent fish!

(*b*) The only good male is a castrated male!

(*c*) Would you care to send a round of cucumber sandwiches up to Room Fourteen, please?

The Sleeper. This man will be found on the banks of shallow lakes and reservoirs, never by rivers where the sound of running water might keep him awake. The Sleeper arrives and sets out his stall: umbrella, chair, tackle box, cheese sandwiches and flask. Then he might, if he's feeling particularly energetic, set up his rod, put a worm on the hook and sling it a few yards out into the water. This done, he can then settle back with a clear conscience, and within minutes he is snoring gently. The first time you notice the end of his rod going you wake him up, but he doesn't appear grateful and you don't do it again. In order that you won't disturb him further he sends the hook out without bait on. Now the fish, and you, will leave him alone, thank God! The Sleeper is the only angler who really means it when he says, 'I'm perfectly happy sitting here all day long catching nothing,' but his stock expression upon waking up is, 'Good heavens! Is that the time?' When you point out to his wife that her husband's approach seems like a waste of time and money she replies, 'Well, we all need a hobby, don't we? And I dread to think what he'd do without his fishing.'

The Creeper. You won't see this one very often, but then that's the way he plans it. The Creeper fishes for brown trout in the clear waters of chalk rivers, and this type of fishing calls for stealth and an ability to flit undetected from bush to reed and back again. Bent double, holding his breath, he scampers about the river bank on tiptoe, looking every inch a DHSS claims inspector. Eyes focussed exclusively on the water he's even been known to 'shush' at a cow chewing the cud in a nearby field. Herons, kingfishers and RAF Phantoms are his natural enemies, and courting couples the major hazard.

Unfortunately some of the The Creeper's angling habits carry over into his everday life. 'Eric! I wish you wouldn't move round the bedroom like that! Fair puts the breeze up me sometimes.'

Although you will rarely see him *in situ*, you might catch a glimpse of him in the library, slinking furtively along the rows, and appearing suddenly every now and again from behind a bookshelf to mutter 'Swoosh!' as he waves his casting arm towards some unsuspecting pensioner.

COARSE ANGLERS

The Youth. The Youth haunts canal banks, but is sometimes found near rivers and lakes. The Youth has pimples, greasy hair, and a stud in one ear. His voice is breaking and shifts from treble to bass and back again as the mood takes it. The Youth is already a good fisherman, probably better than we shall ever be, though we'd never give him the satisfaction of hearing it said. He is earnest and very intense, taking it all very seriously. While his teachers complain about his lack of interest at school and an apparent inability to cope with *Janet and John Book One*, or to string together two sentences in anything other than a grunt, at home he reads all the angling books and periodicals avidly, and can quote up-to-the-minute record lists for coarse, game and sea fish of every westernised country in both hemispheres, *and* tell you what line was used, the bait, the time of day the catch was made, and the last time the successful angler saw the doc about his piles.

Even at this tender age The Youth is in grave danger of being a lifelong bore. He is already a young fogey. The Youth is full of advice. As you kneel on the ground trying to make some sense of a six-inch eel that's wrapped itself round your end-tackle and your neighbour's line rendering the whole issue a dog's breakfast, The Youth will lean over your shoulder, tut-tut, shake his head and begin, 'D'you know, I read somewhere ...' Your reply will not do you any credit.

The Nosher. Sometimes known as Wobblygob! The Nosher never stops eating. He's halfway through his eighth hot pastie of the day when you pick him up outside The Dirty Dog at half-past five in the morning. He will always have the seat next to you on the minibus, and will be tucking in all the way there, talking non-stop and spraying crumbs in all directions. He will also have the peg next to you on a crowded river bank. The Nosher is a confidential talker, which means he leans his head close to yours, giving you a front-row view of whatever he happens to be chewing at the time. You had been looking forward to your own food, but now you're not so sure. Have no fear; it won't be wasted.

'You don't want it? Not feeling too good? I'll have it if you're sure you don't want it. I don't mind helping you out if you're stuck.'

The only consolation about fishing with The Nosher is that he never seems to catch many fish. He's far too busy chomping his way through your lunch to notice that the end of his rod is banging away like the clappers, and you're not going to tell him, are you?

Married Man. Married Man brings his wife with him on a club trip to an away venue. Well, he's not been married too long and doesn't know any better. Now, we don't want to lay ourselves open to charges of male thingy, so let's be quite clear about this: we are *not* talking here about the woman who keeps out of the way and sits in the car/minibus all day long listening to Radio 2 and writing letters to the relatives. Nor indeed do we refer to the wife who genuinely shares everyone's interest in angling and has therefore got all her own tackle and might be a very valued member of the group, willing to sit down and discuss gozzers and breadpaste along with the best of them. No! This woman is the young bride of a few weeks who insists on sitting as close to her husband as she can, almost on his lap, while she tries to figure out what the hell is going on. She is here because she really cannot understand what all the fuss is about. What is it that every Sunday drags him away from their semi on the new Wimpey estate by the marshalling yards?

His motives in agreeing to her accompanying him are mixed. He either

(a) wants to put her off suggesting that she ever come again – 'There you are! I told you it wasn't much fun. You think I'm out here enjoying myself, don't you? Well, now you know better.' Or

(b) He wants to impress. He wishes her to see him in the heroic hunter/breadwinner role he imagines for himself on the one day in the week when he's not trying to sell plastic wine racks to indifferent store buyers. Either way, her presence has a deadening effect on the proceedings. Self-expression is restrained for a start. However, she doesn't last long, poor girl. About a couple of hours is all she can take of the drizzle ruining her make-up, her high heels getting stuck in the mud, and the bloke next along trying to see up her skirt. She retreats to the car, turns the heater on full-fan, so that the battery will be dead when it's time to start for home, and goes to sleep under the dog's blanket.

Match Man. Dour! Very dour is the committed coarse match angler. He's only been known to laugh once. That was the day the crematorium put his Mum's funeral back twenty-four hours due to a double booking, which meant he was free to fish a match on the Wednesday afternoon. He was going to fish anyway, but he'd been a bit concerned that the thought of a near-relative being disposed of ten miles down the road might have affected his concentration.

When it comes to competitions, Match Man is not interested in doing well. Match Man is only ever interested in winning. Fishing is all about coming first, and you can stuff all that guff about companionship and cameraderie, needing a hobby and enjoying yourself.

'We're not here on earth to enjoy ourselves, lad! There's winning matches and dying. It's up to us to get them in t' right order.'

Match Man's approach to winning makes the antics of The America's Cup teams look like the squabbles of a couple of little boys racing rubber duckies in the bath. He knows the rule book backwards, and he's not averse to using it when it suits him, even making it up if it suits him better.

'I think you'll find peg sixty-three is wearing yellow socks, Mr Chairman. He'll have to withdraw.'

'Can't find anything about yellow socks in my book.'

'I think you'll find you're using last year's manual, Mr Chairman. D'you want me to. . .'

'No, no! That won't be necessary. Your objection sustained. 'Course, it'll mean a life ban for the man, but then rules are rules!'

Match Man is an appalling loser. 'I'd have stuffed 'em if they hadn't caught more fish than me. Devious bastards!' And he is not a gracious winner. 'Kiss my boots!'

Specimen Hunter. There's no such thing as an average Specimen Hunter. They're *all* nuts! Specimen Hunter is obsessed with one kind of fish to the virtual exclusion of all others. It's a bit like having a piano and only ever playing one note to try and get it right. And whereas most of us have achieved a fairly competent level of boring when regaling the indifferent with our angling stories, Specimen Hunter wins medals in boring.

'Did you know that carp tend to be solitary in habit except when spawning?'

'Fascinating!'

'Yes! Isn't it? Their natural foods are vegetable matter, small bottom-living creatures, snails, mussels, and tiny larvae sifted from the bottom mud. Bread and worms are popular baits, you know, but maggots or par-boiled potatoes. . .'

Specimen Hunter generally likes to go big, but some do opt for the smaller species, and those so inclined tend to get a bit brassed off when they've gone to the trouble and effort of hooking into a nice perch only to have it snaffled up by a gigantic pike on the draw-in. Not only has the angler lost the very fish he's been after for almost three months, but he's now got to deal with the brute that's just eaten it.

Specimen Hunter has excellent hearing. He can pick up the click of a camera shutter at 800 yards, and he practises his 'modest but delighted' grin for hours in the bathroom mirror every morning.

'What are you doing in there?'

'Smiling.'

'Well, cut it out, you dirty devil, and let somebody else get in!'

The Pessimist. All branches of angling have their harbingers of doom and gloom, but coarse anglers will have to admit they have more than their fair share, and the coarse pessimist is in a class of his own. If he ever did win the big one he'd drop down dead on the bank as they were presenting him with the cheque just so he could say, 'I told you so!' An innocent remark like, 'It's going to be a good day. I can feel it in my bones,' elicits the response, 'Sounds like influenza, lad!'

That spot over there always looks a better bet, but it's no good shifting now because 'some other beggar's bound to get there first'. If it's not raining it soon will be, the maggots will never last out, and it's a well known fact that anglers are 10% more likely to drown in a canal than stamp collectors. The Pessimist is unremitting, and eventually he gets through to everyone. An eager, happy bunch of fishermen, all keenly anticipating the joys of the day ahead, can be reduced to tears in the hour it takes to drive from the corner by the chip shop to the lake, and everybody has a lousy day. Bill's convinced he's never going to catch another fish in his life, Harry's wondering about giving up altogether after hearing what Dave's wife and the milkman got up to while Dave was away fishing that match over Nottingham way, and Tom's pretty sure he must have leprosy.

You will recognise the Pessimist from the look of glum satisfaction on his face, the flat cap, long neck and sticky-out ears. His favourite expressions are;

(*a*) Don't say I didn't warn you!

(*b*) Doubt we'll be able to enjoy ourselves like this after they drop the big one!

(*c*) You have to laugh, don't you!

SEA ANGLERS (Shore fishing)

The Enthusiast. The Enthusiast is getting on a bit in years, and he had a 'condition' which means he's prone to 'turns'. He usually feels a turn coming on at night on the beach, just when the fish are beginning to bite. You have to stop fishing and walk home with him. By the time you return to the beach the tide has turned and is fast disappearing. So are the fish. In spite of his turns The Enthusiast has a ruddy complexion, and he smiles a lot. He is an optimist, and he calls at your home on winter nights when the wind is howling around outside the house, throwing gusts of rain, sleet and hail against the windows. You are snug by the fire when the knock comes on the door, and when you open it The Enthusiast is standing there all geared up. He looks surprised and hurt to see you in your slippers.

'Oh!' he says. 'I thought we was going out.'

'Ah!' you say. 'In view of the weather, I thought...'

'But I got bait,' he says. 'I spent hours diggin' these worms this morning.'

'Ah!' you say.

Now here The Enthusiast has got you. Either way you lose. If you go with him you'll be miserable, cold and wet, and there will be no fish. If you don't go your cosy evening will be ruined because you'll feel guilty sitting by the fire thinking of him out on the beach all by himself. Inevitably you are shamed into accompanying him, because in the final analysis what you're really worried about is what your mates up the pub will say when they hear you let a fellow angler down just because of a bit of inclement weather.

The Enthusiast talks a lot while he's fishing. His favourite phrase is, 'Do you know, I'm perfectly happy standing here all night catching nothing.'

The Moaner. The Moaner is the sea angler's version of the coarse angler's pessimist, though his skills are more sullen and steeped in a philosophical tradition.

'Don't know why I bother really. Been here a full five minutes and I haven't had a bite yet!'

The Moaner will be in his twenties. He works for the Gas Board and his wife is a hairdresser. Nothing is ever right for The Moaner. The weather is too hot/cold, the sea too rough/calm. Whatever bait he's using another would be better. 'These lug are useless. Wish I had crabs.' This elicits a variety of suggestions from fellow anglers, none of which The Moaner finds funny. The Moaner loses a lot of tackle, and he blames everyone but himself for this. He casts. He has forgotten to pull the bail arm over on his fixed-spool reel. There is a loud 'ping' as the line parts and another set of end-tackle wings its way through the air to join countless others, lost forever in the murky depths of the channel.

Moaner: Your fault!
Innocent Bystander: Mine? How d'you make that out then?
Moaner: You was scratchin' yor nose. Broke me concentration, din it?

The Shuffler. The Shuffler can be found on beaches, but is more often to be spotted on piers and harbour walls. The Shuffler is a nosey parker. He's always poking his nose into other people's fishing bags and tackle boxes. His favourite expressions are:
(*a*) 'Ere! Keep an eye on me rod for a minute. Shan't be long.
(*b*) 'Ere! That's a handy looking gadget. Where'd you nick that from then?

The Shuffler stoops, and as his name implies he shuffles everywhere. He wears a dirty macintosh, and has on occasions been mistaken for a flasher. Matter of fact, a Shuffler of my acquaintance was once nearly arrested on a south coast pier. He opened his mac to get out his tobacco tin just as a lady walked by on her regular Sunday morning stroll. This particular Shuffler happened to have his home-made 'priest', a nine-inch length of lead piping hanging from his belt by a piece of string. The poor woman caught only a fleeting glimpse of

this but she screamed. It took three of us
ten minutes to persuade her that the whole
incident was totally innocent and the police
need not be involved. Jim was unimpressed.
As we returned to our rods he muttered,
'Can't see why she wanted to get all worked
up over a little thing like that anyway!'

The Missus. The Missus is never known as anything else
or by any other name. When she first appears on the beach, or
more often the pier, her husband will introduce her, 'Oh, by
the way, lads, meet the missus.'

   No little woman left at home, this one! She's not here for
decoration or out of some kind of wifely curiosity. She's here
to fish. She shares rods with her husband, but she'll do her fair
share of baiting up, filleting, no messing! She rarely talks, but
she does glare a lot. She's not fat, but she is very big. Wide.

She never wears trousers, and even in the bitterest of weather she will have a pullover and a short skirt on under her anorak, and her knees will show round and red raw with cold. The bottom part of her stumpy legs will be thrust aggressively into a fetching pair of short black wellies. The Missus wears vivid red lipstick which looks as though it's been put on with a motorbike!

Her husband is also fairly big, in fact he's a part-time bouncer at The Docker's Club on Saturday nights, but The Missus rules the roost out here on the pier as she does at home. She will often be heard to exclaim, 'Here, you great lummox! Let me do it!' And, as she elbows him aside, 'You? You're about as much use as a chocolate teapot!'

SEA ANGLERS (Charter boats)

The Giver. Of all sea-angling types The Giver is perhaps the most unpleasant. Without fail he catches the best fish of any trip – a 12 lb fighting bass in prime condition, taken on the lightest of tackle, comes on board after an epic battle. The Giver lifts it up ands says casually, 'Anybody want it?'

'Eh?' we all gasp.

'No, go on. Take it. No good to me,' says The Giver. 'I've had better than that.' He turns to the Skipper. 'Remember the one I had last trip, Frank?' (This type always knows the Skipper's name!) 'Now that was a fish that was worth taking home!'

The Taker. The Taker will take anything home. The Taker is always skinny and dark. His favourite phrase is, 'I'll take it if you're sure you don't want it.' He doesn't catch many fish himself, but he invariably leaves the boat dragging behind him several black plastic bags stuffed full of dogfish and other miscellaneous rubbish which nobody else wants. Behind his back The Taker is often a figure of ridicule, which is a shame, for he is basically a gentle person, and probably kind to dogs.

Man's Man. He is hale and hearty, a backslapper and a real good 'chum'. We are all good chums. Man's Man is a joke teller, and his jokes are always long and generally involve subjects such as seasickness and bacon sandwiches.

The Man's Man is not a serious contender in the fish-catching stakes for the simple reason that he suddenly goes deadly quiet about an hour out of harbour. He curls up on a bench with a coat over him, and can be heard gently moaning to himself for the next ten hours until the boat returns to its mooring on the quayside. Then, slightly green about the gills, Man's Man emerges from beneath the coats, belches loudly, congratulates all on board upon a splendid day, says 'We must do it again sometime,' and staggers off along the harbour wall towards The Crown and Anchor where he will spend the evening in the lounge bar telling jokes about seasickness, bacon sandwiches, etc., to another crowd of chums.

The Stern-Jumper. The Stern-Jumper is universally reviled among boat anglers. He will be at the back of a queue of anglers waiting to board a boat, each one hoping that this time they will get one of the coveted positions at the stern. Then, despite having arrived after everyone else, the Stern-Jumper pushes through and down the steps, even elbowing people aside on the boat itself, to get to the best place first. He is extremely thick-skinned, being totally oblivious to protest, insult, and even threat of physical violence. Nobody talks to a Stern-Jumper; he is friendless, a pariah!

The Stern-Jumper can be recognised the instant he arrives on the quayside by his shifty, close-set eyes, his droopy moustache, his greasy hair, and his Tesco's carrier bag. He might possibly be a good fisherman, but he doesn't catch many fish. This is because a surreptitiously held cigarette burns very quickly through nylon line while he's not looking! The Stern-Jumper loses an awful lot of end-tackle. He picks his nose, and hates dogs.

Father. This is the fellow who brings his young teenage son with him. Being anxious to impress the boy, Father swaggers a bit as he moves round the boat, but with no great conviction. He answers the boy's stream of questions in a low, conspiratorial voice, head down, because he has to make a guess at the answers and doesn't want to look silly in front of those who might really know.

Father and son are always seen off from the harbour wall in the early morning by the anxious wife and mother. She waves a tear-stained handkerchief until the boat disappears round the headland, and she will be waiting on the quayside, camera at the ready, when the boat returns in the evening. No one can get off until Father and son have held up every fish on board, and, grinning modest conquering grins, have had their photograph taken by the woman as tears of pride course down her cheeks.

Sailor Sal. Sailor Sal is a thoroughly good type. She is young and fantastically attractive in an outdoor sort of way. Sailor Sal is a student who is travelling the world before resuming studies, and she comes on board because she is somebody's cousin and she's staying with them for a few weeks before moving on. Sailor Sal swears like a trooper, and somehow coming from her it sounds all right. She would never deign to be considered anything other than one of the lads. She livens up proceedings, and she also catches a lot of good fish. When you express surprise at this she will inform you that the last time she was in Australia she worked as a cook on a shark-fishing boat off the Great Barrier Reef. Her biggest catch ever was a 400 lb marlin. She tells you this bit just as your 7 lb bull-huss flops over the side and slumps in an ugly heap onto the deck.

Barnacle Bill. Barnacle Bill would like to be a male version of Sailor Sal. He fails on both counts. Barnacle Bill is a holidaymaker, and this is his first-ever deep-sea fishing trip. He's bought a peaked cap, navy blue with gold plastic flashings just for the occasion. The cap bears the legend 'Skipper's Mate' in discreet white lettering all round the peak. Barnacle Bill says he knows all about boats, and he makes up stories about his sea-faring exploits as he follows the Skipper everywhere, getting in the way and tripping over carefully set rods. But he knows very little about fishing. He cuts himself on a filleting knife, attempts to gaff a little dogfish he's caught and drops the gaff over the side, tries to help with the net and knocks a big bream off the hook of a poor bloke who otherwise hasn't had a bite all day, and gets in the way while a large tope is being boated, thus sustaining painful 'burn' all the way up his arms. Despite all this, and more, he still manages to greet his wife, waiting for him on the quayside, with enthusiasm;

'Wonderful day, dear. You'd have enjoyed it. I showed 'em a thing or two I can tell you. Haven't lost the old touch, you know. Fancy a go tomorrow, dear? Jolly good! What's that, Skipper? No room tomorrow? Oh dear, what a shame. What's that, Skipper? Fully booked for a week? What about next week then? What's that, Skip...? Try the next boat along? He's got vacancies has he? Jolly good! I'll pop along and see him now.'

KNOTS: KEEP IT SIMPLE

'I am a Bear of Very Little Brain,
and long words Bother me.'

(A. A. Milne)

In spite of what he might say when trying to impress, your average angler can't really tell the difference between a turle and a spade-end. But he'll always find himself standing next to someone who can!

As he bends over his line, brow furrowed in concentration, tongue protruding artistically between the teeth, stubby fingers struggling to make a blood-knot look a bit less like something the cat's been playing with, your average angler will become all too well aware of the amused and tolerant sneer of **The Expert**. And in the end The Expert always has to come over. He can't resist it.

'Well that's original. Never seen it done like that before.' Then the sniff. This is followed by a carefully calculated pause, just sufficient in length to emphasise his superiority, before he continues, 'Personally I always use the old double tucked half-blood with Plymouth whipping.'

Now another pause while he awaits the invitation to demonstrate. The pause lengthens as this now becomes a silent battle of wills, but The Expert is a seasoned campaigner, and your average angler experiences the slowly rising tide of dread and panic as the realisation comes to him that he is going to lose again. Eventually, inevitably, he is forced to cough politely and inquire, 'Oh really? How does that one go then?'

Before you can say 'get knotted', The Expert eagerly grabs the two ends of line and his fingers start whizzing round in a blur to the accompaniment of garbled instructions in what sounds like Swahili. Seconds later, movement and commentary cease suddenly, and The Expert holds up the completed article to be admired.

'What d'you reckon then?'

Try to stifle the yawn at this point. And there is no need for a startled gasp of wonder. Sarcasm is lost on The Expert. A muttered 'very impressive' will suffice. But The Expert hasn't finished yet.

'A good little knot that. Tight as a duck's bum! Want me to show you again?'

What The Expert fails to appreciate is that no matter how many times he demonstrates the old double tucked half-blood with Plymouth whipping, your average angler knows he will never understand it. He might, for convention's sake, mumble something to the effect that he's grateful, you've been most kind, much appreciated, I shall certainly use it in future, etc., but he does this only to get rid of this thundering nuisance who won't leave him alone to muddle through.

If things run true to form, the next time he has to tie a knot your average angler will wait until The Expert is busy elsewhere, then he won't be caught out doing things his own way. But in his furtive haste his fumbling fingers will usually manage to make a cock-up of a simple double-granny. Consequently the next tiddler that happens along makes off with the end-tackle and five feet of monofilament as the line parts. The Expert saunters over.

'Hello, hello! What's up?'

'Lost it! Bloody line parted!'

'That's odd. The old double tucked half-blood with Plymouth whipping has never let me down before. Must have been one hell of a fish!'

'Oh it was.'

'Can't understand it. Sorry about that.'

'Think nothing of it.' (Your average angler prides himself on his generosity of spirit.)

'Well never mind, mate. Here, give us that line a second and I'll show you the old full-hitch triple top snap. A nice knot, the old full-hitch triple top snap. Never let you down. Tight as a shanny's fanny!'

In spite of what he might say when trying to impress, your average angler finds the knot sections in angling publications totally incomprehensible. The pictures are enough to put most normal people off for a start. It doesn't matter how clear they try and make the diagrams, they all look as though someone has chucked a plate of spaghetti at a blank sheet of paper. And if the diagrams are difficult to follow then the written instructions that accompany them defy all understanding:

'Pass the end of the line through the eye of the hook, loop and double through. Lay against shank and make a further loop towards the hook bend, bringing the loose end of the line back down to the eye of the shank. Then begin to turn the loose end over the loop, working towards the hook bend, finally pushing the end through the final part of the loop. Moisten and tighten from both ends.
　　A dab of nail varnish helps security.'

A dab of nail varnish? Can you imagine what the wife will say? More important, will she believe you?
　　'Darling!' she calls from the bedroom, 'have you been using my nail varnish again?'
　　'Yes, dear,' you call back.
　　She comes to the bedroom door and gives you one of her funny looks. 'Is the colour all right for you?' she inquires. 'Or should I get the pink-pearl next time?'
　　A dab of nail varnish might be all right for some. No doubt The Expert uses it all the time, but then that's entirely his own affair. Live and let live, I say. My advice: keep it simple. The old double-granny or reef knot may not look very pretty, and you might lose a lot of fish, but on the other hand nobody will be able to refer to you sneeringly as an expert, and you're not complicating matters by laying yourself open to all sorts of equally serious slurs.

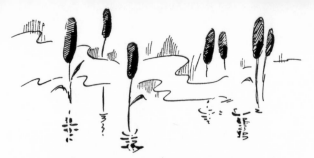

A SCOTTISH
EXPERIENCE

'...those behind cried "Forward!"
And those before cried "Back!"'

(Lord Macaulay)

Scotland. A country road, very early morning, and thick valley mist bringing visibility down to a few yards. A car, its headlights vainly trying to pierce the gloom, pulls quietly into a lay-by. The engine is switched off and the heavy silence is broken only by the muttered consultation between the vehicle's two occupants.

'That must be it.'

'Have another look at the map.'

'Map's no bloody good! This fog's so thick I can't see any landmarks to check with.'

'That bloke in the pub last night said a green gate.'

'Well that's a green gate.'

'In a lay-by, he said.'

'We're in a lay-by!'

'That must be it then.'

'How d'you know?'

'Through the gate, he said. Down the slope, between some trees, over the fence and you come out by the lakeside. Saves driving right round the lake to the car park and having a long walk back.'

'That's what he said.'

'Right! Let's go then, shall we?'

They alight from the car, lock the doors and take their rods, a couple of folding chairs, tackle boxes and packed lunch from the boot.

'Through the gate, a few hundred yards, then the left-hand fork, he said. Can't miss it.'

'Right-hand fork, I thought?'

'We'll check with the map when we get to it.'

'I left it in the car.'

'What?'

'The map.'

'What for?'

'I didn't know we'd need it!'

Ten minutes later they stop, surrounded by tall, closely packed trees dripping with fog.

'My head hurts.'

'Serves you right!'

'Wasn't my fault. They insisted we finish the bottle. An old custom or something. Shows you're friendly.'

'Shows you don't know when to stop! Now, it's got to be this way. He said something about a fence, didn't he? Follow the fence...'

'Over the fence!'

'I'm sure he said follow it.'

'I wish this damned fog would clear. Make things a lot easier.'

'It'll burn away later. When the sun gets right up.'

'Can't see a thing.'

They press on, saturated now by the clinging mist, and sweat-soaked under their coats, the tackle becoming heavier and more awkward.

'Ow!'

'What's up?'

'You trod on my heel!'

'Sorry.'

They stop again.

'We've been here before.'

'What you whispering for?'

'I'm not!'

'Yes you are! What did you say?'

'I said we've been here before.'

'Don't be so daft!'

'I bet we have. Look! That's where I knocked my pipe out against the tree.'

'Bloody hell! I think you're right. If we keep going round in circles like this we'll screw ourselves into the ground!'

'Not doing my head too much good either!'
'Let's go to the right this time, OK?'
'Anything you say.'
And then things begin to look more promising.
'I think we're on the right track. Look! The fence.'
'That's more like it.'
They climb the fence, handing gear over to one another, and begin to wade through thick bracken.
'Along here a bit further.'
'There's the bridge. A concrete bridge, he said.'
'Great! And the railings.'

'He didn't mention railings.'

'Yes he did, didn't he?'

'Don't think so.'

'He must have forgotten.'

'I think we've cracked it.'

'Follow the path round and you come to a low wall right by the lakeside. Fish from the wall.'

'There it is! I can just see the wall.'

'And the lake. Well, the shore anyway.'

Their pace quickened as they approached their destination, the best trout lake for miles around. It's what the hotel brochure promised and all the locals in the pub had confirmed. Within minutes they had tackled up; redworm on size 18 in the water. The chairs were unfolded, they sat comfortably back munching the breakfast rolls left out for them on the hall table, and confidently awaited results.

But after two hours, nothing!

'Not even had a nibble yet.'

'Can't understand it. He said redworm was best, didn't he?'

'Never mind. I think the mist is beginning to shift a bit. The sun'll burn through this lot in no time at all now, and then we can get among them with some flies.'

'Good idea. Pass the flask.'

A short while later and the hot summer sun finally burst through the remaining fragments of thinning mist, which cleared in seconds as though by magic. The sudden change revealed a glorious blue sky, a ring of high, heather-covered mountains, and two anglers sitting by the overflow tank of The Kilfechan Rural District Council Sewage Disposal Works!

A MAN MAY FISH
WITH THAT WORM

*'A Man may fish with that worm
that hath eat of a King, and eat
of the fish that hath fed of that worm.'*

(William Shakespeare)

GAME AND COARSE BAITS

Experts will discuss the relative merits of the wasp grub,
crayfish, elvers, caterpillars, slugs and even the humble prawn.
But basically what we're talking about here are worms and the
simple maggot, bearing in mind that it is to a large extent
coarse anglers with whom we are dealing, and therefore
'simple' is a relative concept.

Maggots. It follows that maggots can't just be maggots! They
are maggots, pinkies, squatts or gozzers, and finally casters.
Well, not actually finally, as those of us who have ever left an
open tin in the kitchen unattended for a few days have found
to our cost. Bluebottles, greenbottles and houseflies on all
surfaces! Whatever you call them, maggots all have the same
sad eyes staring reproachfully up at you as you nick them on
the hook. Now everyone knows that maggots don't have eyes,
and that the two small dots on their backside are breathing
spiracle spots. Everyone knows that! But they still look like
eyes, and you have to feel a certain amount of sympathy for
any creature that has such a sweet-looking face stuck on its
bum. Quite apart from anything else it must be very confusing
for them, especially when it comes to shaving.

Larger maggots can be used as hook bait, while the
smaller ones in any batch will be ground bait. Not much of a
life, is it? On the one hand the sharp end of a size 14, on the
other a joy-ride from a catapult. Either way the end result
leaves a lot to be desired.

At least you don't have to go out and look for maggots.

Anyone returning from a long summer holiday to find the bin-men haven't called for a few weeks can tell you that. Sometimes, though, you do have to go and look for maggots. Several years ago a group of fishermen found themselves on the west coast of Wales, with four days of the holiday to go, having to find an alternative to a sea trip which had been cancelled due to gales. A local lake was the answer, but they had no flies, no maggots, and the nearest tackle shop was twenty miles away. And, being West Wales, it was probably shut! However, the man in the village Post Office came to their aid.

'Couple of dead sheep out on the marshes, boys. Been there for weeks.'

Upshot was, after a lot of strenuous walking and some hilarious activity, they collected a couple of tubs of scrawny-looking maggots which they reckoned would do them for the next day. At opening time in the pub that evening the landlord served them with six pints of the best and innocently inquired, 'So, what have you lads been up to today then?'

'You might not believe this,' one of them replied, 'but we spent the whole afternoon on the marshes, shaking sheep.'

Hearing this, or apparently hearing this, the old boy in the flat cap sitting in the corner slammed his glass on the table in front of him and stumped off into the next room, muttering that they could do without people like that in those parts, and all evening the fishermen got funny looks every time someone from the Public Bar walked through to get to the Gents.

Given the opportunity, it is better to buy maggots from a decent tackle shop. Good variety, reasonable cost, and all the messy part done for you. Did you know, for example, that the ammonia dispelled from the amount of offal required to breed a gallon of bait would keep Duracell Batteries UK Ltd going for weeks? Try keeping that lot in the lean-to and you'll soon find out who your real friends are!

Worms. Again the angler has a choice: buy, breed, or go out and find. Buying has one drawback. It is actually possible to rush into a tackle shop, grab a pot marked 'Brandlings', pay for them and rush out again without checking the contents because your friends are waiting impatiently in the car, engine revving. When you arrive at your destination, a lake up in the hills miles from anywhere, you find you've paid £1.50 for a large tub of excellent garden compost containing not a single worm. You then have to ask yourself which is going to prove the most unpleasant experience; asking the big man in the shop for your money back next day? Or telling your friends, who are busy tackling up, in the next few minutes.

'Dozy pillock!'

'Well, I've got rather a lot on my plate at the moment, what with the Rates, and the Gas, and that bill for the new back door; it's amazing the way they all come in together, isn't it? And then there's ... etc.'

I can't honestly say that I've had fantastic success with breeding worms either. I followed the instructions in the book to the letter, and all went well till I came to the bit which said, 'Then a few weeks later when you require a supply all you have to do is dig in the ground immediately beneath the compost heap where you will find hundreds of worms of various sizes.' I didn't. Five! The rest had done a runner and were probably safely over the border by then.

I once considered emulating the Continentals and
wondered about using bloodworms for the smaller fish on a
local canal. At that time my tackle shop didn't stock
bloodworms so I reached for the book again. 'To obtain and
prepare a supply of bloodworms you need: a pair of waders, a
plastic bucket, a supply of black lawn peat, and the top half of
a lady's nylon stocking.'

This is where I gave up. I got into enough trouble over the
nail varnish (see 'Knots'), and I wasn't going to put myself
through all that again. On reflection I did the right thing since I
subsequently learned that bloodworm should be used on a size
20 hook, or smaller! Now my eyesight's not what it used to be,
and I have difficulty just seeing a size 20 hook these days, let
alone putting a bait on it. And I really hate it when I'm just
congratulating myself on getting a maggot onto a size 18 in
something approaching a reasonable state and some upstart
peers over my shoulder and says, 'I see you prefer to fish big
on this stretch.'

Personally I've got a lot of
time for your common lobworm.
For a start it's big enough to
see without having to worry
about whether you ought to
make another appointment
at the optician's, and
collecting them doesn't
involve using anything
which might lead to the
divorce courts. On the other
hand the man next door
might wonder about
your habit of wandering
up and down the road at
night inspecting the grass
verges with a flashlight,
and he may report you
to the Neighbourhood
Watch.

Luckily I live in the sort of area where if you mention the Neighbourhood Watch to anyone they think you mean the clock in the village Post Office, but the rest of you had better be careful. If you take my advice you'll restrict your nocturnal activities to your own back lawn if you're lucky enough to have one, and if yours is anything like mine the flashlight will be doubly handy, enabling you to avoid the hazards deliberately designed to trap the unwary: scooters, cricket bats, collapsed play-tents, and bikes, all of which have been left out for a rainy day.

Fish. I'm not very keen on live fish being used as bait, though why a live minnow should be any worse than a live crab I couldn't say, unless it's simply that minnows look as though they belong in a Disney cartoon, and crabs are straight out of a cheap horror comic. 'The Creature From The Black Lagoon' sums up just about every crab I've ever had contact with. Apart from this the snap-tackle sometimes used to livebait fish looks so mediaeval when the fish is trussed up in it. There might be a few humans I wouldn't mind seeing try it on for size, but a fish deserves better.

   Deadbait? No real difficulties, though I do sometimes wonder about using a large fresh mackerel to fish for even larger pike. It strikes me that:

(*a*) If you've already got a large fresh mackerel then you've got one in the hand as it were, and ought to be satisfied, but then I enjoy fresh fried mackerel with vinegar and bread and butter. And

(*b*) If you stick it in the water you're in grave danger of actually catching a large pike! Let's be clear about this, specimen pike hunters do have my fullest admiration and sympathy. They can't help it apparently. But not only is the fish they're after at the height of its predatory powers in the depths of mid-winter, involving the angler in long hours out in the freezing weather, but pike can come very big indeed, and a pike's mouth is crammed with hundreds of tiny, sharp, backward-sloping teeth. They also strike me as a fairly bad-tempered species. A fish with all these credentials is one to be avoided as far as I can see. Large pike have been known to feed on frogs and ducks. Any fish capable of this is also well qualified to take a sizeable chunk out of an unwary angler, and I quite like my body the way it is. It may not be pretty, but at least it's all there!

SEA BAITS

The major problem with sea bait is that it bites or it smells. A lot of it does both. However, before it can do either you have to find it.

Lugworm. Lugworm is quite easy. You need a fork, a bucket, a stretch of sand showing a few worm casts, and a friend who's daft enough to believe that you really do have a bad back and that the doctor's told you to do no digging. Lug is fairly harmless. It doesn't bite, and only smells really badly when you've been forgetful and left half a tub outside the back door in the hot sunshine for a few days. You could have sworn that you'd wrapped them up in newspaper, but you realise your mistake the instant you take the lid off and the pong rocks you back on your heels.

Crab. Crab are less easy. I have an aversion to any form of small sea life which can nip. I'm not too keen on larger forms of sea life which hurt either, but at least something like a dogfish will respond to a sharp thud on the head with a rock if it tries to get too friendly with the skin on the back of your hand. Thump a soft-back crab with a rock and you end up with a messy blot on the ground and no bait.

Searching for crabs under rocks and seaweed also makes me feel a bit of an intruder, a voyeur. This is particularly true when I come upon a couple of the little creatures busily engaged in what comes naturally. As I gently lift the top one off his mate I often find myself wondering how I'd feel in similar circumstances. For a crab, 'coitis interruptus' must be a whole new ball game, as they say.

A tub full of crabs brought home for use the following day are in some respects the least offensive of baits as far as the rest of the household are concerned. The children can look at them without making that horrible pretending-to-be-sick noise

that invariably accompanies most other baits when they see
them. The dog leaves them alone after sticking its nose in the
bucket just the one time. The wife can't complain too much
about the smell. On the other hand a bucket of crabs can make
a hell of a din, clacking away for hours on end. You certainly
can't forget where they are. They also have this habit of
ganging together should the opportunity arise to effect a mass
break-out, and opportunities arise frequently in a house full of
children and dogs. Your average crab is not daft!

At the first hint of freedom they don't all hang around
together waiting to be picked up. They scatter to all four
corners of the kitchen. The result is chaos, and since your wife
refuses to go in there until they're all picked up you spend
hours on hands and knees scrabbling around feeling under
cupboards, sinks, cooker and the fridge trying to catch the little
beggars. The children think they're helping by charging round,
shrieking and stepping on some; the dog takes itself off and
curls up under the stairs to sulk; and the wife
stomps off to bed with a hot-water bottle,
muttering something about 'not being able
to take much more of this' and
'telephoning mother in the
morning!'

Ragworm. This species, particularly the King-Rag with its vicious pincers, is a nasty little creature, and is best left to the foolhardy or the masochist. This writer will have no truck with it. His reluctance even to discuss its merits as a bait goes back to his childhood and an incident on Worthing Pier involving a King-Ragworm, some bigger boys, and his trousers.

Squid. I have to confess that I know absolutely nothing about catching fresh squid. You won't find many other authors of a book about fishing prepared to admit they don't know all the answers, but the only squid I've ever come across has been given to me by friends. This usually means it's been frozen, often several times. Even fresh squid tends to honk a bit after only a few hours, so you can imagine what the stale frozen stuff is like. Squid may be an effective bait. Some people swear by it, others at it, particularly when you can't get your rusty, blunt hook through its leathery skin, and more especially when the smell refuses to leave your fingers for weeks, despite regular scrubbings in disinfectant and desperate measures such as rubbing liberal quantities of after-shave over hands and under fingernails. As a bait squid is not recommended for use by waiters or dentists.

Mackerel. Mackerel as a bait is pretty straightforward. You catch it, cut it, and use it. This sounds all right in theory. In practice catching mackerel for bait can lead to ill-feeling, particularly on a deep-sea trip when there aren't too many around. A group which sets off as friends in the early morning determined to share everything, just like always, can become unusually covetous individuals when it gets towards noon and there are only three fresh mackerel left on board to be shared among twelve fishermen. It's at such time you start to remember which mackerel was caught by which angler; also who your real friends are. Will Jim share the one mackerel he's caught with you? Or will he keep it to himself and make you use the evil-smelling stuff in the Skipper's bucket? (Last year's and frozen a few dozen times!)

Mackerel has other drawbacks. I went to the freezer on one occasion in deep midwinter to get out one of several tubs which I had put by in the autumn.

'Where's me mackerel gone?' I called, thrashing about in the bottom of the cabinet. 'I'm going fishing on the beach with the lads. Promised them some mackerel.'

'It's all gone,' said the wife calmly.

'Gone?' I said. 'What d'you mean, gone?'

'Gone!' she replied.

'Gone where?'

'Well, you know it's been a particularly bad winter?'

'Yes,' I said, not sure what this had to do with my disappearing mackerel.

'Well, yesterday while you were at work we had a flock of seagulls in the back garden looking for food.'

I knew what was coming, but there was no harm in asking anyway. 'And?' I asked anyway.

'Well, the children felt sorry for them.'

'I know what's coming,' I said, 'but tell me anyway.'

'Well, the seagulls wouldn't eat the bread we put out for them so I told the kids to try your mackerel. I knew you wouldn't mind, and the seagulls loved it!'

'I bet they did!' I muttered, moving to the window and looking out at the row of fat seagulls perched expectantly along the back fence like a flock of vultures.

I had never thought of my wife as the vindictive sort, but I considered this to be a particularly underhand way of gaining revenge for the incident with the crabs all over the kitchen floor. Yet I said nothing. Your average angler knows when he's licked.

Mackerel also smells. Not as much as squid it must be admitted, but even when relatively fresh it does have a pungent odour not quite all of its own!

Sandeels. We all know that sandeels are netted commercially for sale by professionals, but the angler who wants to catch his own is reduced to scrabbling about for them on hands and knees in the sand just above the water line, using a small hand-fork. There are two dangers inherent in this practice. The first is that you will invariably find yourself in the company of an enthusiast who lashes out with his fork at anything that moves. Sooner or later he will gouge a lump out of your ankle, drawing blood. This hurts. Not only that but the sandfork is covered in accumulated rust and other filthy substances which you dare not guess at, so to be on the safe side you have to drive yourself to hospital where you hang around for hours waiting for a tetanus jab.

'Hello,' says the nurse, voice ringing with indifference. 'What have you been up to then?'

'I was digging in the sand with my friend and he caught me on the ankle with a little fork.'

'Oh well. Whatever turns you on, I suppose. Drop your trousers!'

JAB!

'Aaah!'

'Right. Off you go then. I should stick to playing with your plastic boats in future!'

The second danger associated with getting your own sandeels lies in the body having to deal with unaccustomed exercise. Catching sandeels involves strenuous activity in intensive bursts and should only be undertaken by the fit angler, and as we all know there aren't many of those around. I personally only know one fit angler, and he goes round taking chunks out of people's legs with a fork.

NEEDLE OR FORK ?

Having got your sea bait the next problem lies in presenting it. This isn't really as difficult as the experts would have you believe. You simply stick the bait on the hook and shove the whole issue in the water. Keeping it on the hook is another matter. When I first started I carefully tried to bear in mind the advice I read in a book my Dad bought me: 'The lugworm should be threaded carefully on the hook so that any juices are left intact to seep out invitingly on the sea bed.'

For years I've tried to do this, but despite my best endeavours the juices still insist on spreading out uninvitingly all over my fingers before I can get the bait in the water. My earliest attempts at threading lugworm ended up with them looking like thin brown string wrapped sparingly round a meat hook.

Although I think I may now have almost got the hang of using crabs I still tend to be a trifle squeamish when dealing with them, and I continue to baulk at my friends' lusty exhortations:

'That's it. Break his nippers off!' and 'Go on! Put the hook through his eye socket!'

I really thought I'd found the answer to crab baits when I discovered the method of tying the crab alongside the hook by means of shearing elastic, but even then I had problems. 'Bloody hell!' said Jim. 'Is that going Recorded Delivery or Registered Post?'

Sandeels don't present too many difficulties, though their tendency to snap in two when being used still frozen must present some pretty bizarre sights to the fish they're meant to be attracting.

'Blimey, Fred! What d'you reckon that is then?'

'Don't know, Bert. Looks like something's bitten clean through it and spat it out again.'

'Can't taste much good then, can it? Best leave it alone, eh?'

''Ere! What about this over here?'

'What, that little crab with all the elastic tied round it?'

'Yeah.'

'Naaa! Don't fancy that. Tried one of them once. Played havoc with me dentures.'

'LOVELY'
(F.I.P)
EVADED
19,542 FISH
DIED OF HOOK
PERFORATION AT 93

THE LUNATIC FRINGE

As with all other areas of angling, bait has its lunatic fringe.
We're not talking here of the fly man who experiments with
different coloured feathers on his Little Walter, or the coarse
angler who opts for Caerphilly instead of Cheddar because the
wind has suddenly changed direction. No, we refer to the
fanatics, the ones who love their baits, and if the truth were
known would probably take it as a personal insult if a fish ever
did come along and eat any of it. For example there are those
who talk to their bait as though it was human.

'Come here, my lovely. Don't be shy. Who's going to catch
Daddy a lovely big fish then, eh? No need to be afraid,' they
mutter as they carefully slide a size 3/0 Aberdeen hook up a
lugworm's jacksy!

Then there are those who like to experiment. Whereas most anglers reckon they're being pretty daring by risking a squid and lugworm together, or a maggot and a tiny bloodworm in a cocktail, convinced that they're throwing away two good baits simultaneously instead of the more conventional one at a time, this is small beer to your fanatical bait man. Coarse or sea angler, the fanatic has tried it all in numerous combinations, from winkles baked in a light onion sauce to pickled prunes. His current enthusiasm, which he swears by, is a tasty and foolproof little number: King-Rag marinated in dandelion wine. This, he will explain, is one of his less exotic concoctions.

'Got to keep it simple, mate,' he will say. ''Ere, pass me that tub of sheep droppings, will yer?'

Unfortunately the lunatic fringe bait men never actually catch any fish, but they don't connect this fact to the bait they're using. There is always some other factor to be considered.

'Can't understand it, mate. Haven't had a bite all day long. I've got a lovely bit of pork pie and fried slug on the end there an' all. Must be the wrong time of month, I suppose.'

The real joy for the lunatic fringe bait men is to talk on the subject, and in this at least they have the advantage over the rest of us, for when we've chatted about lugworm for five minutes, or considered the relative merits of Hovis and Sunblest for half an hour, there's generally not a lot left to say on the subject, but the fanatic is able to go on for hours...and hours...and hours.

CALLIONYMUS IYRA

*'I did but taste a little honey with
the end of the rod that was
in my hand (and lo, I must die).'*

(1 Samuel 3:9.)

Jim caught a 'dragonet'. We were fishing light, near a reef out on Cardigan Bay, hoping for black bream which had been reported in the area.

'Hey up!' said Jim. 'Got something!'

'A bream?' we asked expectantly.

'Nah! Nothing excitin'. Feels like a little gurnard, or a crab perhaps. Somethin' like that.'

What appeared was a small, beautiful blue and gold coloured fish with a strange, delicate sail attached to its back.

'What the bloody hell is that?'

'Never seen anything like that before.'

'Better get the glove, Skipper. Just in case.'

We carefully dropped the fish into a bucket of seawater and gathered round to watch it.

'Anyone know what it is?'

'It's on the tip of my tongue, er...'

Eventually Jim plucked up courage, put his hands into the bucket and picked it up. A thick jet of sperm shot all over his hands. It was male, anyway!

'I think the little bugger likes me,' said Jim.

We weighed it. As near as we could tell with any degree of accuracy it was at least 7 oz. Then Jim leant over the side and gently lowered the fish into the sea. After a moment's hesitation it swam away from the boat and then downwards.

At my house that evening Jim and I found the picture we were looking for in, of all places, *The AA Book of the English Countryside*. The fish he had caught was a dragonet.

Next morning Jim had a telephone call from the Skipper.

'You know that fish?'

'Yes.'

'It was a dragonet.'

'I know. We found it in *The AA Book of the English Countryside*.'

'Oh!' said the Skipper. 'Have you got the *Penguin Book of Fishing* by Ted Lamb at home?'

'Yes,' replied Jim. 'But it hasn't got a picture of a dragonet in it. We looked.'

'I know,' said the Skipper. 'But take a look at page 525. The British Record Sea List: Mini-Records up to 1 pound.'

Then he laughed. I could hear the cackling over the telephone from where I was sitting. The phone went dead. Jim came from the hallway, a worried frown on his face.

'Where d'you keep your Penguin book?' he asked.

We went to the bookcase and began to consult the *Penguin Book of Fishing*. We found what we wanted on page 525.

'**Dragonet: (Callionymus Iyra)**...' It told us that since 1976 the British Record had been just over four ounces.

And it still was!

NO LIMIT!

'He smiled and said, "Sir, does your mother
know that you are out?"'

(Rev. R. H. Barnham)

Harry finished work at the garage late; too late to grab a bite to eat at home and then drive miles to his favourite salmon pool. Instead he decided to spend the remaining couple of hours of daylight at Emlyn's trout lake.

He approached the farmhouse along the rutted track, the car rocking from side to side, springs protesting at every pothole. Each time he'd driven along here Harry thought he'd found a better line, but each time he discovered he was wrong. He cursed as a wheel dropped into a large hole which he could have sworn hadn't been there last time, and he bit his tongue as his head jolted and his teeth snapped together. 'Bloody man! Why doesn't he do something about this?'

Harry knocked on the door of the farmhouse and waited. No one came, and there was no frantic barking of dogs from the nearby barn. 'Must be round the back.' He followed the path up the side of the house and rapped loudly on the back door. He peered through the kitchen window. Still no one. Another try at the front door. Evidently the Pritchard clan was not at home.

What to do? The answer was simple: fish now and pay on the way out. Failing that, settle up when he next saw Emlyn in The Dragon. He'd done it before. And he'd leave the car in the farmyard so that Emlyn would know there was somebody up at the lake if he came back.

Ten minutes later Harry rounded the bend in the path and saw immediately that he had the place to himself. It wasn't a large water, but the setting was superb: rocky cliffs and boulders on one side and a gently sloping oak copse on the other, and Harry knew from past experience that the lake was well stocked with large rainbow trout.

Anticipation being half the pleasure of angling he now enjoyed the familiar tingle that crept keenly through him as he selected a fly, a simple Butcher to start with he thought, and moved to the water's edge. His right arm came back, there was the usual soft, comforting 'swish' as he brought the rod forward, accelerating it into a wristy flick at just the right instant. The line snaked out across the water and Harry grunted with satisfaction. Suddenly the garage and the bank manager, the VAT man and the strange knocking noise under the bonnet of Mrs Morgan's Datsun Cherry (still under warranty) didn't seem quite so important. Actually he forgot all about them.

The shadows of the crags lengthened across the water as the sun dipped behind them. Eventually they covered the whole lake and the evening lost some of its warmth. After a couple of hours' fishing Harry had to admit that he wasn't having much success. He'd caught nothing. He'd changed fly patterns, varied his cast, moved round the lake at least a half-dozen times, all to no avail. He'd known for quite some time that it was going to be 'one of those sessions', but he was reluctant to admit it to himself too openly, and although the realisation that it was hopeless had trickled inexorably through him he persevered. 'One last cast. Just in case.' He must have said it fifty times.

Now the light was fading, and it was with reluctance tinged with relief that he left the scene of his failure and his disappointment and began to walk back to the farmhouse. Emlyn was home. The Land Rover was parked in the yard, and he came to answer the knock on the door.

'Saw the car,' he said.

'Yes,' said Harry. 'It's four quid I owe you.' He handed Emlyn a five pound note. Emlyn took it, looked at it.

'Haven't got any change,' he said at last.

'Never mind,' Harry replied. 'Give it to me when you see me.'

Emlyn pocketed the fiver. 'Any luck?' he asked.

'Nothing! Two hours or more and not a thing!'

'Pity,' said Emlyn. He paused, then continued, 'Mind you, I'm not surprised. I emptied it last week.'

Harry couldn't really believe what he'd heard.

'Emptied it?' he managed to croak eventually.

'Aye! Took all the fish out. You know. Wasn't paying. I'm wondering about a few holiday caravans instead. What d'you think?'

'I think I'd better go!' said Harry, and trying to contain his anger he turned on his heels and strode towards his car. Halfway there Emlyn's voice stopped him.

'Hey!'

Harry swung round. 'What?' he demanded sharply, half wondering whether Emlyn was going to offer to do the decent thing.

'Since you didn't catch any...'

'Yes?'

'D'you want some fresh frozen? I've got a freezer full in the barn if you're interested.'

Harry waited.

Emlyn continued, 'Two quid a pound to you!'

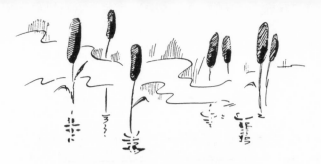

ANN! ANN!

'Ann! Ann! Come as quick as you can!
There's a fish that talks in the frying pan!'

(Walter de la Mare)

***A**dvertisements.* Like the well known phrase, or 'fisherman's fib', some of the advertisements in angling publications can often say one thing but mean something completely different, while many others are just plain daft. The accomplished angler cultivates the habit of questioning claims and reading between the lines. For example:

A SUPERB NEW REEL WITH A MULTIPLICITY OF FUNCTIONS

This means it's got so many unnecessary gadgets you need a degree in engineering to use it effectively. *And* it's expensive!

NORWEGIAN STYLE LODGES RIGHT ON THE BEACH. IDEAL FOR ANGLERS.

This is a hut with an outside loo near Avonmouth Docks. Liable to flood at high tide.

FROZEN SQUID. EXCELLENT RATES FOR BULK PURCHASE.

The Health people have been round following complaints from the neighbours about the smell.

HOTEL ACCOMMODATION AVAILABLE AT HIGH DISCOUNT RATES FOR ANGLING PARTIES.

It's such a grotty place they can't get anybody else to stay there.

A NEW CONCEPT! A ROD THAT IS EQUALLY AT HOME ON BOAT...OR BEACH.

Totally inadequate for either purpose!

SEAFOOD PLATTER AND FRESH SALAD.

A sign outside a pub, it means dogfish and lettuce.

EQUIP YOUR BOAT FOR WRECK FISHING.

We do a nice line in diving equipment, and rescue gear.

FULL SET OF COARSE FISHING TACKLE. GOOD CONDITION GENUINE REASON FOR SALE!

His wife has threatened to leave him if he doesn't pack it in and spend more time at home. Mind you, he had to think twice about it!

FOR SALE. ANGLERS WIGLOO TENT.
USED ONCE. £30.

Never been so uncomfortable in my life!

DAIWA MAGFORCE. FOR ANGLERS WHO'D RATHER
SPEND THEIR TIME FISHING THAN BIRDNESTING.

You mean there are actually some who prefer birdnesting?

MACKEREL TRIPS

Fifty holidaymakers crammed into a boat built for twenty, sharing ten rods and feathering like the clappers for two hours at £3 a throw to take home a dozen 'joeys' between the lot of them.

FOR SALE
RIVERSIDE COTTAGE. FISHING RIGHTS INCLUDED.
BE THE ENVY OF YOUR FRIENDS!

What kind of a short-sighted idiot wants to be the envy of his friends? Your enemies are the bastards you want to get one over on!

FLIES TIED TO YOUR SPECIFICATION.

Tell us what you want. We'll send you what we've got.

SEA GOING CHRONOMETER CHRONOGRAPH.
GUARANTEED WORKING DEPTH OF 100 FEET.

Your sea angler will go to some extreme lengths to catch fish, I know, but this has got to be a joke!

MAKE YOUR OWN PERFECTLY
FINISHED LEADS.

Maim yourself in the comfort of your own home.

GALEORHINUS GALEUS

...'tis bitter cold,
And I am sick at heart.'

(Shakespeare)

It's fairly safe to say that most anglers would subscribe to the cock-up theory of events which shape our ends. The cock-up theory, or 'sod's law', states that if things are going badly they will inevitably get worse.

George is probably the best all-round fisherman I have ever known. His knowledge of all areas of the sport of angling is vast, and his preparations for river, lake, beach or boat are always meticulous. For years he consistently beat the rest of us out of sight for the weight and condition of the fish he caught, whether it was salmon in the Mawddach, pike from Bala Lake, or bass from the beaches of Cardigan Bay.

One summer we decided to give the tope (*galeorhinus galeus*) a bashing, and every weekend would find us out in the bay enthusiastically dropping bait on long traces over the side in the hope of hooking a prize specimen. But try as he might poor George went through almost the whole season without catching a single tope, while all around him were regularly pulling in good ones. On one particular trip a twelve-year-old boy, a novice fisherman on holiday with his parents and anxious to have a go in a boat, brought a beautiful tope of over 40 lb on board.

'Well done, son,' muttered George through gritted teeth, as he helped the boy get the hook from the mouth and return the fish to the sea. It was about this time that the 'mickey-taking' shifted into top gear.

'Hey, George! What was the size of the tope that lad sitting next to you had last month?'

'Sit next to me, George. Please! I haven't had one over thirty pounds for nearly an hour now.'

'You've tried everything else, George. Why don't you send 'em down a menu? Let them choose.'

This went on until the very last tope trip in late September. George realised it was probably his final opportunity since any day now the tope would be leaving the bay to head south. Although he felt a great deal less than optimistic George went through his usual meticulous routine: he tackled up with a long wire trace, a brand new hook recently sharpened, a carefully cut 'flapper' of fresh mackerel, and then he settled back to wait. He was next to me on the boat, and I watched him doze off in the late September heat. Suddenly he jerked upright at the sound of line stripping from his reel. He leapt to his feet.

'Easy now,' I heard him mutter to himself. 'Let him go for a while.'

He began to apply the brake gently, the fish came back towards the boat and George took up the slack. Then it was away again and he let it have its head, but as the fish turned for a second time George struck! It was a big one. In an instant the rod bent almost double. Meanwhile the rest of us moved quickly to get tackle inboard to avoid the risk of tangling. Then we stood on the seats to watch and encourage, genuinely pleased and appreciating the look of concentration mingled with joy on our friend's face as he felt the surge of power through the line.

The fish dived again towards the stern of the boat and George followed it, shuffling along the deck, his rod dipping over the gunwales, the tip waving frantically like a twig in a gale.

And then suddenly it was gone! The line went abruptly slack and George staggered backwards. There was silence for a few seconds, then 'Lost him!' George cursed loudly. 'Bloody lost him! Bloody line snapped!'

'Must have scraped the bottom of the boat,' said the Skipper. 'It happens.'

George reeled in and the end of his line appeared above the water, waving in the slight breeze. He reached out and grasped the end, drawing it close to inspect it, and we all gathered round, prepared to commiserate. But then George's eyes opened wide with horror and disbelief as he saw the little squiggles curling round like a pig's tail, irrefutable evidence of a badly tied knot parting under pressure. Even worse for George, we also had seen it!

'Hey, look at this, lads,' called out Jim to anyone who was still not looking. 'We always said old George likes to give the fish a sporting chance.'

'Gone a bit far this time, if you ask me,' said Jack examining the line.

'Who's going to take a long time to live this one down then, eh, George?' said Jim with undisguised delight.

George raised his eyes to heavens as the implications for the months ahead began to dawn on him.

'All season you've waited for that fish, George,' mused the Skipper, 'and then you of all people go and cock it up like that! It's a funny old game!'

LET THY SPEECH BE SHORT

'Let thy speech be short,
Comprehending much in few words.'

(Ecclesiasticus 32:8)

Whatever else he is, and he is a lot of things, your average angler is a master of the final word; sometimes intentionally, often not!

'Can't sell you permits for that stretch, Sir,' said the man in the shop. 'It's syndicated.'

'Must be all the fluoride they keep bunging in it,' said Albert.

It was unfortunate, but it was accidental. Bob's cast had taken his line into the next man's swim, and the fellow jumped up, red-faced and furious, yelling 'My water! My water!' Bob shrugged apologetically, then the end of his reel jerked suddenly and he began to draw carefully towards the bank the largest carp any of us had seen in ages. 'My fish! My fish!' he called back sweetly.

It was Jack's turn to buy the day tickets, but he was hanging back as usual. 'I wouldn't say he's exactly tight,' Sid murmured in my ear, 'more cross-threaded!'

Jim and I watched in amazement as a novice fisherman jerked a tiny gurnard on board with such ferocity that the fish, end-tackle and several metres of line flew backwards over the boat. As it went the angler spun round with it, the line wrapped itself round his chest and neck, and he finally ended up pinned against the wheelhouse door, arms splayed out, his sleeves entangled in the lengths of mackerel lines hanging from the rack. Jim looked carefully at the poor fellow as he hung there; then he blinked, sniffed, turned back to his rod and muttered, 'What a bleedin' awful way to spend Easter!'

Our local vicar is a fanatical salmon fisherman. Even so, I was surprised to find him in the river one Sunday evening when I arrived.

'Didn't expect to find you here, Geoff,' I called. 'Not on a Sunday.'

'Nothing in the Good Book says I can't fish on a Sunday,' he called back. 'Just so long as I don't enjoy it!'

DAI'S ARMY

'A Company for carrying on
an undertaking of Great Advantage,
but none to know what it is!'

(South Sea Company Prospectus)

I'm Wilf Williams,' said the old man. 'And this old crock is
Gareth Jones.'

Gareth waved his walking stick in greeting and David
nodded back.

'Just moved into the village?' asked Wilf.

'That's right,' David replied.

'Writer?'

'Yes. Freelance.'

'We all have a cross to bear!' grunted Wilf.

'Fisherman?' Gareth inquired.

'Whenever I get the chance. Fly mostly.'

'Nobody's perfect!' Wilf grunted again.

A pause.

'We're thinking of fishing the bridge tonight,' said Gareth.
'Do you fancy it?'

'Well, yes. Yes I do,' replied David. 'Thanks.' The bridge
would be new ground, and even in the short time he'd been in
the village he'd heard good things about it.

'We can lend you a bit of tackle,' said Gareth.

'I'd appreciate that,' said David.

'Need some bait,' wheezed Wilf. 'Sandeels, lug. You'll have
to give us a hand with that bit. The old trouble, you know.'

'Trouble?' asked David.

'Heart!' whispered Gareth, loudly confidential.

'I see,' said David.

Wilf tapped his chest to let David know where his heart
was.

'Doc says my chest is a timebomb, doesn't he, Gareth?'

'His very words, Wilf.'

'And Gareth's not much use with his leg,' Wilf continued. 'So...'

'Fine,' said David, taking his cue. 'Bait it is. Just tell me when and where, and I'll meet you.'

They were waiting for him, lying on their backs in the sand dunes, flat caps pulled over their faces to shade them from the baking sun. Wilf stood and looked across the estuary which was emptying of water as the tide went out. He sniffed. 'Sandeels first!' he muttered, and he led the way from the dunes onto the harder sand at the water's edge. 'This'll do!' Then with an energy that belied their years and infirmities he and Gareth dropped suddenly to their knees and began to work feverishly at the sand with small forks, yelling encouragement to each other as they splashed about in the shallows, scraping and scooping up the tiny darting fish. David watched in amazement as the two old men, whooping and hollering like little boys, half filled a small bucket in a matter of minutes. They stopped as abruptly as they had begun. Gareth straightened up and, gasping, he limped towards David, deposited the bucket at his feet, then collapsed onto the sand muttering, 'It's gone again! Gone again! Oh my God, why do I do it?'

Meanwhile Wilf was still kneeling in the shallows, slowly thumping his chest, mouth open, making small gurgling noises, eyes glazed. David didn't know which one to turn to first. He ran to Wilf. At least Gareth was on dry land.

'Are you all right? What can I do?'

Wilf closed his eyes, shook his head. He opened and shut his mouth several times without uttering a sound and waved David away, giving him what he probably imagined to be a reassuring grin, but in fact grimacing and distorting his features horribly. David returned to Gareth who was now upright again, swinging his bad leg to and fro, shaking his head, rolling his eyes heavenward and clicking his tongue. Eventually Wilf came to join them; his face ashen, hands on hips, he gulped in great mouthfuls of air.

'By God!' he gasped. 'That was a near thing. Thought I'd gone that time.'

David was still worried. 'Look,' he said, 'we've got to get you home as soon as you're ready to move. Have you got pills or something you can take?'

'Can't go yet,' said Wilf. 'Haven't got the lugworms!'

'But neither of you is in any fit state to dig worms,' insisted David. 'I'm going to get you back right now!'

'Nonsense!' said Gareth. 'That was nothing. About par for the course that. You should see it when either of us really has a bad turn.'

'Lug beds are this way,' said Wilf, and they began to shuffle off across the sand. 'You'll have to do this bit, David,' he called over his shoulder. 'Bring the fork, there's a good lad!'

The bridge was a wooden structure, an old viaduct really, about half a mile in length, and it traversed the estuary a mile inland from the sea. That evening they reached its middle span after a desperately slow walk from the village, during which David realised that he had somehow become responsible for carrying not only his own, but most of his two companions' fishing gear as well. There was plenty of light left as they tackled up, the sun on their backs still well above the horizon as they faced inland towards the mountains. Gareth showed David how they prepared for the bridge, with a long trace and a sandeel threaded on a hook and kept firmly in place by gently winding shirring elastic round bait and hook.

'Current gets pretty strong,' said Gareth by way of explanation.

'We fish the tide coming in from this side of the bridge,' said Wilf. 'The flood takes the traces upstream, away from the bridge piles. Then when the tide turns and starts to run the other way we cross over and fish from the other side. Handy, eh?'

As dusk fell they were joined on the bridge by other small groups of anglers, calling out greetings before they too settled down in their favourite spots along its length. It wasn't much time before the first catches were being made: flounder and plaice, dogfish and bass. And then it was dark and lamps were lit.

It was getting towards midnight, just before the high water slack, when David became aware of a buzz of information being passed along from group to group. Gareth stumped towards him.

'Dick the Nose!' he said.

'Beg pardon?' said David.

'Dick the Nose!' repeated Gareth. 'Owen Richardson, the water bailiff. He's on the bridge.'

A few minutes later David turned to see an imposing figure arrive in the light of their glowing lamp. He was over six feet tall, carried a large salmon rod, and was wearing waders. He stopped, there was a pause while he adjusted his eyes to the light, then he swore.

'Bloody hell!' he said. 'That's all I need! Dai's Army out in full strength. Both of 'em!'

'Evening, Dick,' said Wilf sweetly. 'Enjoying yourself?'

'So far, yes. But I now confidently expect the evening to run rapidly downhill!'

'You old flatterer, Dick,' said Gareth.

'And who's this?' the bailiff asked, nodding in David's direction. 'A new recruit?'

'Haven't you met our David?' inquired Wilf. 'He's a new boy on the bridge. We're just showing him the ropes.'

David took the proffered hand. 'Owen Richardson,' said the man. 'Nice to meet you, David. And if you should be in need of any advice the most important thing to remember is to get shot of these two characters as soon as possible!'

David grinned. 'I'll try and remember that,' he said, 'but it's not been too bad so far.'

'Oh, it gets worse, David. It gets worse, believe me!' He turned back to Wilf and Gareth. 'Now then, you two, I suppose it's pointless my asking a simple question such as "Have you any unauthorised salmon or sea-trout in your bags" because I know I shan't get a sensible answer.'

'Salmon?' Wilf considered. 'Er...only two tonight, isn't it, Gareth?'

'No, no,' Gareth replied, gravely shaking his head. 'You're wrong there, Wilf. It's three salmon, two sea-trout.'

'Come to think of it, you could be right, Gareth. I was beginning to lose count.'

'Idiots!' muttered Richardson. 'Still, I suppose I'd better take a look in your bags.'

THE
GETS-UP-YOUR-NOSE
UNAUTHORISED
FISH BAG

He bent
over Gareth's
fishing bag.
As he opened
it Gareth
gasped loudly,
guiltily, and Richardson looked quickly up
at him. Gareth smiled down on the bailiff,
and slowly winked at him. Richardson muttered
something under his breath before moving on to
look through Wilf's bag. He straightened up.

'What about your bag, David?'

'I haven't got one yet,' David replied. 'I'm sharing theirs.'

'I see. Right. That's it then. All clean.'

'I do believe we've just spoilt his evening again, Wilf,'
Gareth chuckled.

'I'd like to think so, Gareth,' replied Wilf.

'Idiots!' Richardson muttered again. 'One of these days,
boys. One of these days.' Then with a long sigh and a shake of
his head he wandered off into the darkness.

'Well!' exclaimed David. 'What on earth was all that
about?'

'That? Oh that was just Dick doing his job,' chuckled
Wilf.

'No. All that business about salmon, sea-trout?'

'Oh, that! Yes, it's possible,' said Wilf. 'They both pass under the bridge on their way upriver. There are some very famous stretches the other side of Dolford. People come miles and pay the earth to fish them.'

'But has anyone ever caught a salmon from the bridge?'

'I've seen a few taken in my time,' Wilf continued. 'And sea-trout. Mind you, I've never had one yet, but if I ever do young Dicky will be the last to know about it!'

It was several weeks later that David next met Owen Richardson. On one of his rare excursions to the nearby town David heard his name being called and he turned to find the bailiff approaching him across the road.

'David? It is you, isn't it?'

'That's right. Er...?'

'Owen Richardson. Water bailiff.'

'I remember, yes. Of course. On the bridge. But what a good memory you must have. The light wasn't all that good as I recollect.'

'Ha! That's part of the job. See a new face in the area, stick it at the back for future reference. And how are our two friends? Seen much of them lately?'

'Occasionally. They're fine.'

'Good, good. They're not bad old boys really. It's just that they do have this ability to get right up my nose! I don't get down your way very often, and when I do it's only to show my face for appearances' sake. I know there's rarely anything untoward going on in that patch. And yet, every time I see those two I have this strange feeling that they're getting one over on me. Why is that, d'you suppose?'

David laughed. 'I think it's just a knack they have. It's something they've cultivated over the years to fit in with their incorrigible image. They think it suits them. I'm sure it's nothing personal.'

'You could be right,' Richardson said. 'I shan't lose any sleep over it, but just once I'd love to catch them up to some no good, if for no other reason than it might take the knowing grin off their faces every time we meet!'

That summer proved to be long and warm, and while David settled down among his new neighbours and his work began to go well, he also continued to fish regularly with Wilf and Gareth. He dug their worms, collected their crabs, frequently carried their gear over long distances. In return all their favourite haunts became familiar to him: the most productive stretches of the open beach, the rocks under the cliffs, the pools at The Point, the favoured sections of the harbour wall. While he sometimes found himself missing the gentle artistry of his first love, the fly, David also had to admit that he was enjoying his new-found knowledge. And there were several trips to the bridge, of course, though no further sightings of Dick the Nose.

A fine evening in late September found the three fishing on the bridge again. The setting sun threw a red and gold glow over the water as the estuary filled to near capacity at the top of the tide. In half an hour it would be slack and the flow would begin to go the other way as the vast bowl gradually emptied back into the ocean. It had been a very quiet few hours. Gareth had caught a small plaice at the start, but since then nothing, despite several changes of tackle and the occasional substitution of prawns for sandeels. Now all three leaned on the railings enjoying the view and the torpor induced by inactivity. David was humming to himself as he idly watched the water running clean and clear over the gravel patches under the bridge.

Wilf suddenly lunged for his rod as line began stripping from his reel. 'By God, I'm into something here!' he gasped. 'It's a fighter!'

David and Gareth moved quickly to join him, and their eyes followed his line down into the water. There was a splash of something silver as the fish leapt out of the water and crashed down again.

'A bass?' David suggested.

'It's a big one if it is!' grunted Wilf, letting out some line.

The fish broke the surface again, leaping completely clear of the water this time before falling back.

'Salmon!' yelled Gareth. 'It's salmon!'

'Shut up! Shut up!' hissed Wilf between gasps. 'We don't want everyone to know.'

'I think it may be a bit late for that,' said David, fully aware of the stir that all this activity was creating among the other groups of anglers on the bridge, many of whom were leaning far out over the railings and looking in Wilf's direction.

'That's the trouble with fishermen!' gasped Wilf. 'Damn nosey lot they can be!'

'Give it some line! Give it some line!' advised Gareth urgently.

'I know! I know! What d'you think I'm trying to do? Pillock!'

'That's not very nice,' said Gareth. 'I was only...'

'Gareth!' panted Wilf. 'This is not the time to come over all precious on me! Oh God, I think me arms are dropping off!'

'Ah!' said David, suddenly becoming aware of the strain showing on Wilf's reddening face. 'Look, do you think perhaps I'd better...?'

'No bloody fear!' growled Wilf. 'This one is all bloody mine! Even if I have to die for it.'

'It might yet come to that!' thought David.

'It's coming. Get the drop net down there. Quick!'

Eventually the fish came to the surface beneath them, tiring rapidly now, but still struggling. David lowered the drop net, Gareth leaned out over the rail and grasped the line to help Wilf manoeuvre the catch into it. They began to haul the net up, and soon it was over the rail and deposited gently on the bridge planking. Flapping in the net was a huge, silver salmon. Wilf sank back against the bridge railings, breathing heavily.

'It is my opinion, boys,' he gasped, 'that an experience like that knocks even sex into a cocked hat!'

'How would you know?' demanded Gareth. 'It's been so long you've forgotten!'

The news of the salmon spread quickly along the bridge, and then news of a less welcome kind filtered back the other way.

'Oh my God!' muttered Gareth. 'That's torn it.'

'What's up?' asked Wilf who was down on his knees having dispatched the fish. He struggled to his feet with the salmon in his arms.

'Owen Richardson! He's just come onto the far end of the bridge.'

'I don't suppose there's the remotest chance that you've purchased a salmon licence recently?' asked David.

'Daft bugger!' grunted Wilf. 'Here! Who's going to hold this fish for me?' He began to chuckle. Gareth also found this remark funny and joined in.

'What are you going to do?' asked David. He at least could feel the beginnings of panic in the pit of his stomach.

'Look,' said Wilf, 'go and meet him, Davey. Stall him a bit. Talk to him.'

'But what shall I say?'

'Anything! Just go towards him for God's sake!'

David left them and sauntered in what he hoped was a convincingly casual manner towards the approaching water bailiff.

'Evening, David,' called Richardson as he drew near.

'Ah! Hello there, Owen,' gulped David. 'Um...how are you?'

'Fine. And yourself?'

'Oh, can't complain, you know. Can't complain.'

'Good, good.' Richardson paused before continuing his walk. 'Any luck this evening?'

'No!' answered David very quickly. 'Well...not personally, that is...I mean, not me. Us. Nothing to speak of.'

'Never mind. It's early yet.' Richardson stopped as he saw Wilf and Gareth leaning casually over the bridge railings. 'Oh, what a lovely surprise. Good evening, men.'

'Ah! Hello, Mr Richardson,' Wilf greeted him. 'How nice.'

'What a pleasant surprise, Mr Richardson,' said Gareth. 'Lovely evening for it.'

'Quite!' replied Richardson, a puzzled look on his face as he studied them both carefully. 'So gentlemen...any sea-trout tonight? Perhaps the odd salmon or two, eh?'

'Not a thing, Mr Richardson.'

'Very quiet night so far.'

'Just one of those nights, I guess, Mr Richardson.'

'What? Nothing at all?' Richardson's eyes opened wide in mock horror. 'But, er...aren't you even going to take the piss, lads? Don't disappoint me completely. Not after so many happy years together.'

Wilf was shocked. 'Good Lord, Mr Richardson, we wouldn't do a thing like that! Would we, Gareth?'

'Wouldn't dream of it, Wilf.'

Richardson looked carefully again from one to the other, then very slowly said, 'D'you know, boys, if I were a suspicious man, I really do think I would have to take a little peek in your bags.'

'Mr Richardson! Really!' Wilf was indignant. 'That's not necessary. You know us. Always clean as a whistle.'

But Richardson was already rummaging through Wilf's bag.

'Nothing there.' He moved to Gareth's and repeated the process. 'This one's all right.' He stood up and looked at David, who suddenly felt himself colouring. They couldn't have, he thought. They wouldn't!

'And yours, David?' Richardson asked. 'You have one now, do you?'

'Yes,' said David, his voice a disconcerting squeak. 'That one.' He watched, heart pounding as Richardson searched through the contents thoroughly, and then David breathed an audible sigh of relief as the bailiff rose to announce, 'Also clean!'

'Ah well,' Richardson continued. 'That's it then. Best be off. Right. Never mind, lads. Better luck next time. Keep trying.'

'And you, Mr Richardson,' said Wilf.

'Some people just never get the luck they deserve, I expect, Mr Richardson.'

With a grunt, and one last lingering look at the two old men who returned his stare with faces registering blank innocence, Owen Richardson moved on.

'Right!' said Wilf, beginning to bustle about, 'I don't know about you two, but I've had enough excitement for one night. Let's away to the pub, shall we?'

'I think you're right, Wilf,' Gareth agreed. 'We don't want to push our luck, do we?'

'Hang on a minute!' said David. 'Hang on!'

'Yes?' asked Wilf.

'Well...for a start,' David pointed out, 'for a start the tide's only just going slack...'

'And?' demanded Gareth.

'And second...' David dropped his voice. 'What the hell have you done with that fish?'

'Right! That's what we'll do then, boys,' said Wilf very quickly and in a loud voice. 'There'll be other nights. The pub it is then, eh?' And then more quietly, having looked around to ensure they could not be overheard, he whispered to David, 'I owe you one!'

'Sorry?'

'I said I owe you the first one.'

'Why?' asked David, also whispering now.

'Because,' murmured Wilf, 'when you pick up your coat off the deck, be careful! There's a nice fat salmon wrapped up in it.'

'What?' gasped David, appalled at what they had done.

'Oh, I shouldn't worry, Davey boy,' said Gareth. 'You've got an honest face. You'd have been all right. And anyhow, we would have appeared as character witnesses for you in court!'

'I don't see you around much with our two friends these days,' Owen Richardson remarked as he and David sat by the log fire in the bar, enjoying a whisky to keep out the winter chill. 'Seen the error of your ways?'

'Something like that,' David replied.

'Or was it the error of their ways, eh?'

'You know how it is.'

'Well, yes. I think you're wise.' Richardson leaned closer and continued confidentially, 'You know, I still get that inane grinning every time I meet them on the bridge. Always as though there was something I didn't know. But one of these days they'll overstep the mark. Then I shall have them!'

'Really?'

'Oh yes. I can smell an illegal fish from a mile away.'

'Can you?'

'Absolutely! I'm as good at that as I am at remembering faces!'

'HOOKS'

A NEW DRAMA SERIES
COMING TO YOUR TELEVISION SCREENS
SOON

A searing story of love at first sight as Clive Brown and Lady Fiona Stanton bump into each other outside the tackle shop.

'Sorry, lass!'

'No, no. 'Twas my fault. Oh dear, I appear to have squashed your parcel.'

'Nowt but a few brandlings, lass.'

'But it's made a dreadful mess of your cardigan.'

'It'll all come out in t'wash.'

'Oh, you are brilliant! I wish I'd been brilliant enough to think of a brilliant answer like that.'

ANGLING INQUIRER

'WE ARE JUST GOOD FISHERMENS FRIENDS' SAYS FIONA

SEE PAGES 1–57

A tragic tale of family loyalties stretched to extremes.

'I'm not best pleased, lad.'

'But why, father?'

'The Stantons are a game family, lad. Always have been, always will be. What do they know of the hardships involved in trying to raise a large family of maggots from little eggs, eh? Nay, lad. Best leave well alone. Know your place.'

'But I love her, father.'

'You love her father? By heck, lad! You're not going all funny on me, are you?'

A chronicle of conflict.

'Good God, Fiona! A coarse man? Why don't you go the whole hog and pick a sea angler?'

'Now you're just being silly, Daddy!'

A clash of two worlds.

'I understand you want my daughter, young man?'

'That's right, Sir.'

'You realise of course there may be...difficulties?'

'Yes, Sir. But I've talked my father round and he says he's willing to put up with having a game angler's daughter in the family as long as the neighbours don't get to hear!'

A collision of cultures.

'Harriet, the boy's a bounder! Caught a twenty pounder, had his photo taken, then he put the bloody thing back in the river! Just won't do!'

'Old habits die hard, Cranleigh. The boy's got to learn.'

'But everyone knows it's fish for the table first, and the leftovers shared out among the tenant oiks down in the village!'

Meanwhile Lord Stanton's gamekeeper, Travers, harbours secret longings of his own.

'Every time I see one of those beauties jump the wier, Molly, I can't help but think of where they do come from.'

'What, like Harrods?'

'No, Moll! The sea, the sea!'

'Now you hush up, Raymond Travers, d'you hear me? Don't you ever let the master hear you talking like that. He'd confiscate your terminal tackle without a second thought, and then where would we be?'

And Lord Stanton's younger brother, Sir James Plowman-Stanton, MP, has problems.

'Sea angling, Harry? I'd rather die first!'

'It's the boundary changes, Sir James. Come the next election you'll have Throgbenton Housing Estate. Your flies won't do you much good up there. That's lug country!'

'But Harry, I couldn't possibly. There's family honour at stake here, and some things are more important than self-interest, surely? I mean, what about principles? No, I'm sorry, but I won't compromise my principles!'

'So you don't like being an MP, Sir James?'

'Right then, Harry! Let's see if I've got it now. This is a fourteen foot beachcaster, right? And this thingy is a Clement's Boom.'

'Correct, Sir James!'

Unaware of his wife's continuing torrid affair with the man in the local tackle shop.

'Oh, Des!'

'Oh, Lady Plowman-Stanton!'

'Oh, Des!'

'Oh, Lady Plowman-Stanton!'

'Oh, Des! That was wonderful. I have this tingling sensation running up my spine.'

'You're lying on my display of pike lures, Lady Plowman-Stanton! Or may I call you Clarissa?'

'No, you may not! That would be getting far too familiar!'

An affair which handsome young Doctor Freddy Proctor, erstwhile suitor to Lady Fiona, feels he must bring to the attention of Lord Stanton.

'My Lord, the man's even been known to fish for... It's no good. I can't bring myself to say it!'

'Get on with it, Proctor, you idiot! Dammit man, my daughter's been seduced by a coarse angler! There's nothing you can tell me will be worse than that.'

'This man, my Lord...'

'Well...?'

'He's been known to fish for...for...prize-money!'

'Bloody hell! Is this possible?'

''Fraid so, my Lord.'

'I see. Look, be a good chap and ring for Standish. Tell him to get in here chop-chop and pick Lady Stanton up orf the floor!'

Will Fiona finally finish with Freddy and get all coarse with Clive?
Will Des break it off when Sir James calls in to purchase his first filleting knife?
Is Molly fair game?
Will Travers finally succumb to his dark desires, declare himself, and join the rabble-rousing revolutionaries on the pier?

'HOOKS'!

You will thrill to the stunts.

'Now then, Jervais, what I want you to do, love, is wade downstream a bit, waving your rod about, then I want you to slip on an unseen rock and fall flat on your face in the water. Splosh! Just like that. Get it?'

'It'll ruin the make-up, Dicky. Couldn't we get a stuntman to do this bit?'

'Jervais, you are the stuntman!'

Marvel at the costumes.

'This olive green looks awfully drab as a ballgown, Deirdre. Frightfully *démodé!*'

'But it's so you, Maria, darling. It matches your complexion exactly.'
'Bitch!'

Hum the tunes.
'Blimey, Steven, couldn't you have come up with something more original than Handel's 'Water Music'?

Gasp at the spectacle.
'Now, I want all you lot on this side of the bank to stick your tongues out at all those on the other side, then you lot all throw bread paste back at them!'

Weep buckets...
'D'you want this rubbish on, Terry?'
'No, love. Switch over. It's nearly time for 'Neighbours' on the other side.'

UNLUCKY ESCAPE

Mr David Martin, 37, a news-agent, of Thrumpton Lane, Retford, Notts, who jumped into the River Idle to escape a swarm of wasps while out walking with his dog, was bitten on the leg by a pike.

The Daily Telegraph, Thursday September 6, 1988.

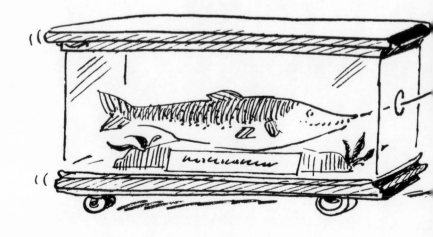